SECRETS OF SIX-FIGURE WOMEN

ALSO BY BARBARA STANNY

Prince Charming Isn't Coming:
How Women Get Smart About Money

SECRETS OF
SIX-FIGURE
WOMEN

SURPRISING STRATEGIES TO
UP YOUR EARNINGS
AND CHANGE YOUR LIFE

BARBARA STANNY

HARPERCOLLINS *Publishers*

HarperCollins books may be purchased for educational, business,
or sales promotional use. For information please write:
Special Markets Department, HarperCollins Publishers Inc.,
10 East 53rd Street, New York, NY 10022.

FIRST EDITION

Designed by Jennifer Ann Daddio

Library of Congress Cataloging-in-Publication Data
Stanny, Barbara.
Secrets of six-figure women: surprising strategies to up your
earnings and change your life/by Barbara Stanny.
p. cm.
ISBN 0-06-018548-1
1. Wages–Women. 2. Women executives–Salaries, etc. 3. Women
in the professions–Salaries, etc. 4. Women–Employment.
5. Career development. 6. Success in business.
I. Title: Secrets of 6-figure women. II. Title

HD6061 .S73 2002
650.1'2'082–dc21   2002017251

02 03 04 05 06 QW 10 9 8 7 6 5 4 3 2 1

For my parents,

DICK AND ANNETTE BLOCH.

I love you.

Education is not the filling of a pail, but the lighting of a fire.

—WILLIAM BUTLER YEATS

CONTENTS

ACKNOWLEDGMENTS

From the moment this book was conceived, a multitude of angels came into my life. I lovingly and gratefully thank all of you.

Thank you, Candice Fuhrman, my wonderful agent and friend, for planting the seed that would blossom into this book and for your unwavering support throughout the process.

Thank you, Diane Reverand, for seeing the potential when no one else did. Lisa Berkowitz, my savvy editor, I can't thank you enough for adopting this project with such genuine enthusiasm. Working with you has been a joy.

Thank you, Doris Ober, for your skillful pruning and shaping, your perceptive critiques, and your priceless encouragement. I couldn't have done this without you!

Thank you, Beena Kamlani, for your uncanny ability to tidy up the clutter and whittle down the excess. You are truly a gift. As are you, Arlene Mikelsons. Thank you for meticulously, efficiently typing the transcripts and dropping them off at my door along with a basket of freshly laid eggs.

Thank you, my amazing referral network, especially Stuart Williams, Susan Davis, Karen Page, Gayla Kraetsch Hartsough, Eileen Michaels, Dee Lee, Pamela Ayo Yetunde, and Karen McCall. When I was at my wit's end, wondering how the hell I would ever find enough women to interview, you blessed me with more names than I could ever use.

Thank you, Cal, for being such a great husband, for patiently reading my rambling first drafts, for always knowing just when I needed a hug or a head rub, and, most of all, for taking me to Mexico to write the last chapter. Once again, you kept me balanced throughout.

Thank you, Melissa, Julie, and Anna, my beautiful daughters, for your constant, caring inquiries into my progress and for your obvious pride in my success. Melissa, thank you for your excellent feedback.

Above all, thank you, six-figure women. Many of you are mentioned by name, while some preferred anonymity. My conversations with you inspired me in ways I hadn't expected. As others read your stories, I suspect they'll say the same.

And Carruch, thank you for everything!

WELCOME TO THE ERA
OF THE
SIX-FIGURE WOMAN

The king was in his countinghouse
Counting out his money;
The queen was in the parlor
eating bread and honey."
—"SING A SONG OF SIXPENCE"

THE NEW BREED

I'll never forget, some years back, when a friend called me with shocking news. She had just learned she had to pay $250,000 in income taxes.

"Why so much?" I had asked in amazement. Then she told me what she had earned the previous year.

She may have been stunned by her tax bill, but I was even more stunned by her earnings. I had never known a woman who made so much money. Back then, she hadn't, either. But these days, her income isn't so uncommon—not by a long shot. Women today are not only stepping out of the parlor but also raking in the profits. Never before have we seen so many women forging such lucrative careers, even in fields you'd never expect. These high earners include entrepreneurs, corporate executives, professionals, and, believe it or not, part-timers. Not only that, women's chances of high incomes are increasing faster than men's. From 1996 to 1998, according to a study by the Spectrem Group, the number of female high earners shot up 68 percent; the number of males in that category increased by only 36 percent.

It's a fact. We've entered the era of the six-figure woman. Yet the remarkable progress of these high earners has been surprisingly low profile. Why? In large part because until recently they didn't exist. "It is only in the last two decades that women have had [substantial] personal earnings from their own activities," reports a 1999 study by Deloitte Touche.

And such women are still a minority. Fewer than 20 percent of six-figure earners are female. Most women remain sorely underpaid. According to the Department of Labor, the average woman brought home less than $25,000 in 1999. In virtually every field, women make 50 to 80 percent of what men make.

THE INSPIRATION

I have always been among the majority, a card-carrying underearner, a poorly paid writer only dimly aware of this new breed of women. So when my agent, Candice Fuhrman, called early one January morning, eager to tell me her idea for this book, my immediate reaction was decidedly negative.

"Why not interview women making a lot of money, six figures or more?" Candice exclaimed over the phone. "It must be the first time in history we've had so many—"

Before she finished the sentence, I had dismissed her suggestion. How boring, I thought. And, yes, intimidating. I pictured these high-earning women as cold, tough, aloof, hard-driven, designer-dressed people I could never relate to, leagues above me.

Then suddenly, I stopped dead in my tracks, staring straight at the misshapen ghost of my financial past. What was I telling myself? Could this be why I never made much money? How could I let myself bring in big bucks if I had such a disparaging view of those who were doing it? Within seconds, more questions flooded my brain. Was holding a high-paying job even worth what I imagined it would entail? Did six-figure women have to work absurdly long hours, forfeit their femininity, forgo their happiness, give up all semblance of a personal life? Did their marriages hold up? Did their children suffer? Did they bear lasting scars from breaking glass ceilings or battling gender bias? Was it possible for *anyone* to become a high earner? Could I? All these thoughts raced through my mind at lightning speed while I was still on the phone with my agent.

"I would love to know more about these women," I heard Candice saying.

"I would, too," I found myself agreeing. And, in a very brief span of time, what began as an unappealing idea had turned into a personally compelling and totally captivating project.

But as soon as I hung up with Candice, the devilish critic that lives in my head began spewing forth its own set of questions. "Don't you see how you're setting yourself up for failure by aiming for the unattainable?" the critic insisted, never one to mince words. "How the hell are you ever going to find six-figure women to interview?" And, of course, the critic sneered, "Who are you to even think you could fit in this category?"

It was time for a reality check. I called four friends who I suspected were financially successful. I requested an interview and asked them for names of other high earners, and then asked the women whom they referred me to for other names. Some of them sent

word of my project to their vast e-mail lists, and suddenly perfect
strangers were showing up on my cyberspace doorstep. Before I
was through I had talked to more than 150 high earners. I was
absolutely floored by the enthusiastic support I received from
them, most of whom I never met. As busy as they were, each one
talked with me for at least an hour, usually over the phone, frequently more than once.

I asked questions about their upbringings and lifestyles, their
dreams and disappointments, their successes and setbacks, and the
reasons for their financial achievements. They were surprisingly
candid about such intimate subjects and were earnestly reflective in
their responses. Why did they agree to the interview? I asked. As a
way to help others, nearly everyone told me. But they were also getting something in return. "I've never really had a chance to talk
about these things," one woman confided. Most seemed to agree:
Talking openly about one's income is still considered taboo. Oh sure,
women moan and groan freely about how little they make. But how
often do they wax on about their rising wages?

LEARNING FROM OTHERS

I know, from prior experience, that the best way to learn anything
new is to study those who are already succeeding at it. I learned to
manage my finances that way, by talking to women who were smart
investors for a project I was hired to do, years ago, as a freelance
writer. My book *Prince Charming Isn't Coming: How Women Get
Smart About Money* is based on those interviews. And that book
spawned a whole new career for me, teaching women what I had
learned.

Up until those interviews, however, I was financially oblivious. I voraciously clung to my father's worldview: Managing money is clearly a man's job. I was too ignorant and scared to believe otherwise. And since my father was the founder of H&R Block, the nation's largest tax service, I figured he should know. My first husband, however, turned out to be a lousy Prince Charming, losing a fortune (of my trust fund) in reckless investments. After our divorce, he left the country, leaving me to deal with colossal tax bills, three small children, and a brain incapable of deciphering financial jargon. But those conversations with financially savvy women changed everything. I now invest with confidence.

Could I become a high earner the same way—by talking to women who were already there? Until I began toying with the idea for this book, I had never even thought to ask the question, never even entertained the possibility. Earning six figures was as far-fetched as a time, years before, when my father had stood in my kitchen and threatened to take away my trust fund if my husband couldn't manage it better. Tears streaming down my cheeks, I vividly remember screaming, "Why can't I manage it?" In the next second, my father and I just stared at each other, both of us incredulous, struck by how ridiculous a notion that was.

Fast-forward fifteen years, and earning six figures seemed equally, if not more, ridiculous. (After all, I'm a writer. Everyone knows that most writers don't earn much.) And to be honest, earning my own livelihood, outside my investments, had always felt just beyond my reach, an impossible feat that left me with interminable insecurity all my life (a classic symptom of inherited wealth).

I knew there were others who felt exactly the same way, for all kinds of reasons: some because they came from wealth, but many more because they lived in lack. I had spent the last several years traveling across the country and speaking at conferences, meeting countless women. I was struck by how many were living paycheck to paycheck, struggling to get by on salaries so measly they could barely make ends meet, let alone scrape up enough spare cash for a mutual fund. Even a few extra dollars was beyond some women's scope. So many of them, like myself at one time, never let themselves aspire to making top dollar, never even thought it was possible, or if they did, had no idea how to make it happen.

Just recently a woman came up to me after a speech I gave. "I really want to start investing," she said earnestly, "but I have trouble scrounging up enough just to cover the basics."

When I suggested she might consider *earning* more, she just sighed. "I'd love to, but how? I don't want to go back to school. I'm hoping something will just pop up and grab me."

This conversation was remarkable only in its unremarkableness. Since I wrote my first book, I've witnessed an incredible surge of interest among women in the area of investing. Women are pouring their money into the stock market and their hearts into learning about it. But I've been equally struck by the level of passivity and resignation when it comes to their wages. I've yet to attend a women's conference that includes a workshop on increasing income, and I seldom hear women even discussing that possibility. No matter how deep their financial holes, most women never consider higher pay as a viable way out. Over and over again, I hear the same words: "I'd like to make more money, but . . ." Only the excuses vary: no time, no energy, no chance, no clue. The list goes on. Their holes get deeper.

For far too many women, their financial limits have become a fact of life. The thought of making more is like climbing Mount Everest, a colossal, if not impossible, task. They may have the desire, but they lack the hope or belief in themselves to meet the challenge.

That's exactly how I used to feel. But all that has changed since

I learned the secrets of the six-figure women I interviewed. My income soared before I even finished writing the book.

THE OTHER SIDE OF THE COIN

I didn't just interview high earners. I also talked to women in the opposite camp, those who were making well below their earning potential. As you might expect, I had no problem finding plenty of women who fit this criterion. Again, I began by contacting friends, talking to them on the phone or over lunch. I also began offering workshops I called "Overcoming Underearning" in my hometown. (These groups were invaluable in helping me integrate the lessons I was learning from six-figure women and figure out how to apply them in real life.) The underearners I spoke to, whether one-on-one or in our groups, were equally enthusiastic and open about sharing their experiences. (More about underearners in chapter 2.)

I wanted to know why these women—often bright, talented, and equally qualified as those making more—were struggling financially. Was it because they chose lower-paying jobs, took more time off for family, lacked experience in the workforce? Or had they simply joined the female masses in jobs with fewer raises, smaller bonuses, and less frequent promotions? Were there certain qualities high earners possessed that they didn't? Could these low earners start making more if they knew how? Or had the financial chasm between the sexes become so insidious and tenacious that even presidential warnings, congressional action, media outcry, women working men's jobs, individual activism, and organizational pressure from groups like NOW and Catalyst, which are devoted to equal pay for equal work, have been unable to shrink it significantly?

As Thomas J. Stanley and William D. Danko, the authors of the runaway bestseller *The Millionaire Next Door* declared, after extensive research: *"All the odds are against women earning high incomes."* The *Washington Post* agreed: "The wage gap is proving to be one of the most enduring barriers to women's economic equity."

BEATING THE ODDS

Well, here's a seven-figure question: *Why, in the face of such formidable odds and enduring barriers, are there millions of women actually making big money?*

As I've come to see, the real problem is this: We've been paying way too much attention to the wage gap and not enough to wage gains. What if we shifted the spotlight from women's plight to women's progress? What if we turned our attention from what's wrong with the system and instead analyzed what's working for those who are succeeding? We're not ignoring the problem; we're merely shifting our perspective.

"Obviously there are barriers to advancement," explains Carol Gallagher, coauthor of *Going to the Top*. "But if we focus on the barriers, we're more likely to encounter them. We achieve what we focus on."

This book is meant to help us shift our focus from the income barriers to the women themselves who are breaking those barriers. We may not put an end to global disparity, but we might find ways to improve our own personal landscape. Even if we can't eliminate economic inequality altogether, we can at least work to tilt the odds in our favor, bump up our earnings, and build up our assets. If enough of us do that work, who knows what ripple effect it will have?

My express purpose in writing this book is this: *to identify the secrets of six-figure women and come up with some straightforward strategies for applying those secrets to our own situations.* The whole point of *Secrets of Six-Figure Women* is to offer insight, hope, and guidance to any of you who aspire to earn more, regardless of how little you're currently making, or, for those of you already in the six-figure range, or close to it, to provide an opportunity to learn from others sitting in the same boat.

LIFE-ALTERING LESSONS

What I learned from these conversations was life changing for me, as I hope it will be for you.

- Above all, I learned that it's entirely possible for any one of us, with average intelligence, to increase our income without selling our soul. No matter how difficult your circumstances or how discouraged you feel, climbing the salary scale is entirely within your grasp.
- While not all jobs can turn into six-figure ones, there are many ways to raise your standard of living without sacrificing, but rather *enhancing*, your quality of life.
- Hefty incomes don't guarantee a happy life, or even peace of mind. Some six-figure women feel neither satisfied nor secure, but they are a decided minority. The majority are contented. These successful high earners have the most to teach us.
- There are certain requisite traits every successful high earner possesses that are available to anyone. (These traits are discussed in chapter 3.)

- When you deliberately hone or rigorously fine-tune these requisite traits, you automatically set in motion a process that
  will increase your income.

It became clear quite early in my interviews that six-figure
women, regardless of how varied their occupations or disparate their
backgrounds, pursued a surprisingly similar path to financial success. Each woman, at critical moments in her career, took a certain
action or performed a particular task that involved one of the traits
required for financial success. I began to see that these comparable
actions or tasks were in fact actual strategies, and that virtually
every woman employed the same seven ones (which are fully
explained in chapters 4 through 10). As I began consciously culti-
vating each of the strategies I heard these women talk about, I suddenly, remarkably, found myself earning more than I ever believed
possible. The strategies were like compass points for me. They put
me on track and kept me on target. I feel confident they will do the
same for you.

In fact, just as I was about finished writing this book, I got a call
from a friend, Stacy Ferratti, who is a corporate trainer.

"I wanted to let you know that last year I earned $105,000," she
exclaimed proudly. It had been almost a year since we'd talked at
length, over a leisurely lunch, about the strategies I was learning
from my interviews.

"How did you do it?" I asked eagerly.

"It just sort of happened," Stacy replied. But I knew better. As
her story unfolded, I heard how she applied each of the strategies
outlined in this book. However, what really hit home was a comment
she made. "Until we talked about being a woman who earns
$100,000 or more, it hadn't really occurred to me to focus on that or
believe it was even in reach. The whole idea seemed so pie-in-the-

sky. But when you asked me why I wasn't earning more, it was like you opened up a groove in my brain."

AT THE HEART OF THE MATTER

This book is meant to open up a groove in your brain, to persuade you to stop settling for less and start opting for more. And I'm not talking just about money. In the course of employing the strategies, you will likely observe that something else is also occurring—you're not only boosting your income but also personally growing in a very deep way.

It's been true in my own experience and I've repeatedly heard the same from others. The six-figure women I interviewed often spoke more animatedly about their private awakening than their financial advancement, about discovering the essence of who they are, the meaning and purpose for their lives, and expanding the boundaries that had limited not only their livelihood but their entire existence as well.

Numerous psychologists have told me that the amount people earn indicates how they feel about themselves, like a mirror reflecting back their level of self-worth. But in my interviews, I wasn't clear which came first. Did people make more because they felt good about themselves, or did they feel good about themselves because they were paid more? Most of the women I talked to reported that as their earnings soared so did their self-esteem.

"When I made money it changed the way I thought about myself," one woman asserted. "I'm worth more. I had money to prove it. Success is a wonderful feeling." Another likened money to a barometer. "I made $150,000 so far this year, which tells me people think I'm talented. When I wasn't making money, I would say,

'Steph, you're so talented you should have more clients.' But it wouldn't help. I didn't feel worthy. Making this kind of money feeds my self-esteem."

It certainly worked that way for me.

I still cringe when I recall all those years sitting across from my accountant at tax time, hearing him laugh when he got to my income. "The government is going to think this is a hobby," he would snicker. It was humiliating, though I pretended it didn't matter and actually berated myself for even making money a focus. But when my accountant suggested I incorporate this year because of the amount I had earned, I can't tell you what it did for my confidence, or how much more secure I felt knowing that if anything happened to my husband, my family, or my investments, I could take care of myself. I felt exactly like the woman who announced during our interview, "Just saying I'm prosperous makes my shoulders go up a little straighter."

Straighter shoulders are really what making six figures is all about: not the zeros on our paychecks, but the impact on our psyches. As an article about successful women in *Fortune* magazine put it, "It may sound New Age, but high-powered women want work that allows them to realize their full selves." That's precisely what I heard from six-figure women. Their pursuit of greater profit triggered a personal evolution. Some even referred to it as a spiritual quest of recapturing (or discovering) their dreams, living fuller lives.

"When I started this work," said a latecomer to six figures, "My only regret was, Why didn't I find this years ago? This is truly what I was born to do. If I didn't make a dime, I'd still do exactly what I'm doing."

This book will take you down a path not well marked by precedent and introduce you to other women, like yourself, who have traveled the path and reaped the profits. You may notice, as you stand at the entry point, the words of philosopher Thomas Carlyle inscribed like an oracle portending the outcome: "Let each become what [s]he is capable of being." In this spirit, we turn the page, and perhaps a new leaf, to uncover the secrets of six-figure women. The time has come for you to discover your potential, increase your prosperity, and pave the way for future generations. The fact that you're reading this book tells me you're up for the challenge. Let's begin.

1

THE QUEENS IN THE
COUNTINGHOUSE

I believe the power to make money is a gift from God.
—JOHN D. ROCKEFELLER

Money is congealed energy, and releasing it releases life's possibilities.
—JOSEPH CAMPBELL

I began my interviews with two broad questions in mind. What were six-figure women really like? And what did it take to make that much money? Our conversations were fascinating and, in many ways, eye-opening. I was reminded of the "surprise balls" my parents used to put in my stocking at Christmas. I'd unravel the layers and little gifts would appear. That's precisely what happened during my interviews. As I began peeling back emotional layers, I discovered all sorts of surprising revelations. For starters, I realized those off-putting images I held of highfliers were nowhere near the actual truth. These women were not intimidating at all. They were personable, likable, and actually pretty much like all the other working-women I know—trying to make a living, trying to get ahead in their careers, and trying to squeeze in a life outside of work. Some were doing it better than others.

What set them apart from the rest of us, of course, is that they made more money. A lot more. Their combined average income was close to $500,000. Individually, their annual earnings ranged from $100,000 to $7 million. The majority, however, hovered somewhere between $200,000 and $800,000 a year. Most of them had far surpassed their parents' earnings. I heard from more than one: "I make more money in a year than my father did in his whole life." And if they were married (85 percent of the women I interviewed were), the vast majority outearned their husbands. (This is actually above average for dual-career couples. According to the Department of Labor, one in every three working wives makes more than her spouse.)

For some of these women, making six figures was a nonevent. "I guess I didn't really think anything about it, because it's sort of the norm when you graduate from business school," explained Celeste Chang, an investment banker. For others, those extra zeros became a validating, and often exhilarating, milestone. Corporate executive Stephanie French at first dismissed her high salary as no big deal. "So many women make six figures, it doesn't even sound like financial success," she said. But after a brief pause, she recanted. "Actually, I remember the first time I hit that mark, and when people on my staff do—it's like, Wow!"

And still others I spoke to never ever expected to be in this league. "I was absolutely amazed," exclaimed Lucy Tomassi, a bank senior vice president. "I grew up on a dairy farm in Wisconsin, and the idea that anybody would pay me this much money was incredible to me." Lucy, now forty-five, was in her thirties when she crossed into six-figure territory, the average age for most of these women to start pulling in that amount. But I also interviewed women who didn't begin making six figures until they were well into their forties, fifties, even sixties.

During my interviews, I got to see firsthand what the feminine face of financial success actually looks like. Here's what I found.

SIX-FIGURE FEMALES—NOT AN EXCLUSIVE CLUB

As one would expect, there are certain fields where you're more likely to come across six-figure women than others. I had no trouble finding investment bankers, financial advisers, doctors, and lawyers who were making big money. But what fascinated me most were those women working in occupations you wouldn't ordinarily equate with high pay. And surprisingly, there were quite a few of them, from artists to actors, from writers to teachers, from musicians to—get this—a matchmaker, and even a psychic.

Among the high earners with impressive credentials and advanced degrees, everyone swore her education was responsible for her financial success. "The fact I had Harvard on my résumé got me this job. Definitely," an executive stated emphatically. "That education's been good for my self-esteem. It's opened a lot of doors. I know people in ways that I never would have otherwise. When I advise people now, I tell them to go for the best education they can get."

But for all the M.B.A.'s and Ph.D.'s I spoke to, I also talked to scores of women whose only credential was a bachelor of arts or a two-year associate's degree. And, surprisingly, there were a number who had no college degree at all, some of whom were high school dropouts. What's more, the lack of credentials didn't seem to hurt them one bit.

"Credentials? You can hire credentials!" exclaimed a financial executive who has an undergraduate degree in classical civilizations. "I didn't want an M.B.A. I was scared it would homogenize me in some way. But almost everyone I've worked with told me, 'Frances, you've got to get credentials.' You know something? I've surpassed most of them."

Entrepreneur Kitty Stuart, a seventh-grade dropout, actually sees an advantage in her lack of education. "Because I didn't know any better, I went out and tried things people said I could never do."

Not having a degree didn't stop Karen Sheridan, either. She went from being a full-time, middle-aged housewife to a six-figure earner in four years—without any college. "I couldn't go to school. I was supporting a family. So I had to learn on the job." Those jobs included stints at Touche Ross, one of the big-five accounting firms; at Capital Trust, selling money management services to pension funds; and at Bank of New York in a senior executive position. She finally enrolled in college and earned a degree in her fifties, long after she had entered six-figure country.

"How did you get all those jobs without a college degree?" I asked in amazement.

"I never brought it up and they never brought it up, either," she said, laughing.

Women like Frances, Karen, and Kitty share a well kept six-figure secret:

Financial Success Is Possible in Almost Any Field, and

Lack of Education Doesn't Have to Hold You Back.

Admittedly, there are a number of careers, say kindergarten teacher or Christian missionary, where you're not going to make six figures or anywhere close to it, no matter how hard you try. Still, I found enough highly paid women who were once in low-paying jobs or worked in fields that aren't normally high-paying to know this: *We may not all make six figures, but there's no reason why any ordinary woman can't be making an above-average salary if that's what she wants.* And doing so is much more in our control than most of us realize.

WOMEN AT WORK

When I told New York real estate tycoon Leslie Wohlman Himmel the title of this book, she burst out laughing. "I have no secrets," she chortled. "I'm no genius. I just work really, really hard."

If there's one hallmark for high earners, it's that they're exceptionally hard workers. I wasn't surprised. I expected these six-figure women to be slaves to their jobs. But hard work has many faces and, like success itself, means different things to different people. As I came to see, the critical factor is not the number of hours as much as the intensity of focus.

"I don't work hard," Nicole Young, a senior vice president of Charles Schwab, told me. "Working hard has a negative connotation. I'm not making any sacrifice. I get to do the best work of my life. I love what I do. I work passionately, not hard." But others fit my stereotype to a T, flat out admitting they worked way too much. In many cases, I had difficulty telling where their work stopped and their personal life began. And so did they.

"A lot of people think it's extremely glamorous because I can make my own hours," events planner Stephanie Astic said. "But everything I do is related to my work. Everything. From the moment I wake up until I go to sleep at night, every day, every weekend I'm working. When I'm on a project, I sleep it, I breathe it, I eat it."

I suddenly flashed back to a recent interview I'd had with another business owner who was in tears the entire time. "I've been crying for two days straight," this woman told me between sobs. "I'm sick of this business. I'm working way too hard, making less money, and having no fun." Was Stephanie following in her footsteps?

"Are you ever afraid you'll burn out?" I asked, knowing she'd been at it more than eight years.

"I'm very careful of that. Whenever I have downtime, I really shut down," she responded thoughtfully. "I try to go away three or four times a year, Florida for a few days, Puerto Rico, or someplace where I can turn off, sit in the sun, and do nothing."

Here's where I began to notice that the women I was interviewing were falling into two groups. One group, the Successful High Earners (SHEs), like Stephanie, loved what they did, worked passionately but sensibly, consciously striving for (though not always perfectly achieving) some semblance of balance.

The other, smaller group were what I called the Hard-Driven High Earners (HHEs). These were superwomen on steroids, examples of ambition spun out of control. They often hadn't a clue how many hours they worked; they just knew how few hours they slept. Like the woman who cried throughout the interview, these hard chargers will break down before they'll slow down, and even then, they'll often force themselves to keep plugging away. They may have once loved their job, but by the time I caught up with them, their passion had turned to obsession, their work had become an addiction, their long hours felt more like hard labor, and their generous salaries were but golden shackles.

"Why don't you quit?" I asked one thirty-year-old woman who admitted she was sick and tired, literally, of her high-pressured job.

"The money makes it hard to leave," she confessed. "It's like heroin. You get addicted. It's not just the compensation. It's the lifestyle, the opportunities, the experiences, and the people you're exposed to. You get used to a certain way of life you don't want to give up."

But money isn't the only reason some high earners have lopsided lives. Overwork has become an occupational hazard for ambitious women trying to make it in a man's world. As The *St. Louis Post-Dispatch* succinctly summed it up, "Women have to make disproportionate sacrifices to compete equally in the work world." Many weary women told me they have to work twice as hard as the men just to keep up. It's an easy, perhaps inevitable, trap to fall into, but the SHEs get out before it's too late.

Jenna Graham, who was employed by one of the largest technology companies in the world, is one who didn't. "I was one of the very few women executives," she told me. "I worked eighteen hours a day. I'd come home at midnight and work until two a.m. I couldn't just be equal, I had to stay ahead of the men. When I did have relationships, they didn't last because work got in the way." Eventually, overwork took its toll.

"I went home one day, and didn't go back. I sat in my house for a month, and one day my sister came and said, 'Something is really wrong with you.' And the next thing I knew I was in a hospital. And you know what? The company sent me a six-figure bonus check, but I never got a card."

Jenna's story is an example of what can happen when a woman becomes too single-minded and obsessed with her job. The good news is, if my interviews are any indication, a growing number of HHEs are wising up (or wearing out) and choosing to work smarter, not longer. They watch for signs of strain and consciously reduce their speed before they crash and burn, doing whatever it takes to find a rhythm of working that fits their temperament, their values, and their preferred way of life. They'll make changes in their current job, switch companies, or start their own. These women have discovered an important secret for achieving success and staying sane:

Working Hard Doesn't Mean Working All the Time.

Lisbeth (Beth) Wiley Chapman learned this the hard way. "Breast cancer was the excuse I needed to say no," she told me.

"You make a lot of different decisions if you have a life-threatening illness."

For this energetic fifty-eight-year-old entrepreneur, a public relations consultant for financial firms, cutting back included moving from downtown Boston to the more serene shores of Cape Cod. She bought a cottage near the beach, slashed her hours from seventy to thirty a week, and, amazingly, her income soared.

"I work very hard from nine to noon," she said. "Then I have lunch on my deck, look at the birds, and from one to two, I watch a soap opera while I read my mail. Then maybe I'll work two more hours. I discovered, if I'm efficient and focused, I don't really need to put in all those hours."

I was genuinely surprised at how many women, like Beth, were actually able to make more money working fewer hours. They were living proof that *it is possible to pare down your hours and at the same time actually pump up your income.*

"I put in eighteen years and horrendously long hours at Dupont," Linda Giering, now vice president of a medical education firm, told me. "It never paid off. I didn't get the salary or responsibility I wanted." So Linda switched companies, cut her hours to no more than forty-five a week, and negotiated a much higher salary. "Overwork is a self-inflicted punishment. I don't do that anymore."

This theme of working less and making more was especially true among the entrepreneurs. Not so much in their early years of doing business, but eventually many of them came to the same conclusion.

"I consciously made a decision not to let work overtake my life," consultant Carol Anderson told me, which, for her, meant forty hours, four days a week. "I've increased my income by seventy thousand dollars so far this year by doing less work and getting paid more. I don't have to work sixty hours a week unless I tell myself a story." She had also taken two months off to travel to

Nepal, and when she returned, business began pouring in "like I was never gone."

With each interview, my preconceived notions of frazzled workaholics began to evaporate. *It was the intensity of focus on their work, not the number of hours they spent doing it, that factored so heavily into these women's financial success.*

What drove them to work so hard? Ironically, it was seldom the money.

WHAT DRIVES SIX-FIGURE WOMEN

"I was never after the big bucks," Jenna said. "I wanted the recognition and the reward of doing a good job."

Her response reflected another recurring theme among Successful High Earners. With rare exceptions, every woman vowed it wasn't the money per se that motivated her success. It was something much deeper, more personal, and very individual.

This theme emerged in the very first interview I did for this book. I had met Gail Sturm, senior director of Cushman & Wakefield Real Estate, at a conference. She's a stunning woman, personable, feminine, and ambitious. I assumed she had gotten into her field for financial reasons. "I never went into commercial real estate for the money. Never," she said emphatically. "But when the money started coming in, half a million a year, I had an immediate sense of freedom, knowing I can take care of myself and shape my life. Money's never driven me. What drives me is freedom, autonomy, and choices. I never want to feel trapped."

I heard variations of Gail's reaction in just about every conversation I had. Money was not the motivator—it was what money represented. These women were driven more by what they hoped to achieve than what they aspired to earn. Each woman had her own definition of what the money symbolized and what achievement meant.

"If money isn't your goal," I'd ask, "what is?" Their answers were as varied as their hairstyles.

- College professor Vivian Carpenter: "To be economically safe, to have enough money to take care of myself."
- Management consultant Gayla Kraetsch Hartsough: "To do interesting things, to feel good about what I'm doing."
- Financial educator Dee Lee: "To wake up and really want to go to work."
- Restaurant owner Judy Wicks: "To use my talents to serve others."
- Corporate executive Linda Giering: "To be recognized for doing a good job."
- Interior decorator Connie Tsu: "To be famous, to have people know who I am."
- Investment banker Michele Rousselot: "To be in a challenging, exciting environment."
- Marketing consultant Marci Blaze: "To be comfortable enough to care for myself and help others."

The common strand that ran through each response was an important secret these women discovered for becoming a truly successful high earner:

Focus on Fulfilling Your Values Rather Than Financial Gain.

Each one had a vision for her life based on cherished values like recognition, security, challenge, or independence. These intangible goals, more than hard cash, provided the fuel for their financial success. Money became the by-product of their value-based ambition and, simultaneously, gave them more opportunities to live out their authentic values.

"Money was not a goal," said one woman. "I was driven to be self-sufficient. My mom's been married four times. I saw her dependency on the next relationship for her livelihood. I never wanted to do that."

Almost every woman I interviewed expressed a genuine longing to live life on her own terms, and that desire—be it for autonomy or achievement, for happiness or fame—imbued her with a wellspring of raw energy that kept pushing her higher and higher. Otherwise, as several found out, striving solely for money is like a steady diet of pizza or pastry. After a while, you're left craving for more.

In fact, one woman took me to task for my focus on six figures. "I know you're writing about financial success and making money. Frankly, I'm a little uncomfortable with that," restaurateur Traci Des Jardins chided me. "If I had a fifteen-year-old daughter trying to figure out what she wanted to be and all she wanted was to make money, that would really scare me. I hope my kids don't grow up with that being their only focus."

When I asked her why she felt that way, she replied, "If making money is the goal, you'll never make enough to be happy. You'll always want more. A lot of people fall into this trap and never find happiness because they're always chasing dollars."

LOVE RULES!

Very few of the high earners I spoke with were chasing the dollars. But make no mistake: They fully intended to be well compensated for exercising their talents in *jobs they enjoyed*. "What's important," one declared, "is to follow my heart."

There was near unanimous agreement on this. As a result, just about every one I spoke to really loved what she did for a living. From what I saw, this passion for her work played a much more significant role in a woman's success than any impressive credential or high-flying career. This became one of the most valuable secrets I learned:

Loving *What You Do Is Much More Important Than* What *You Do.*

"If you're not passionate, you shouldn't be doing it," events planner Stephanie Astic declared. "I think passion is more important than what field you're in, more important than hard work," echoed consultant Carol Anderson. "Yes, I work hard, but I love what I do. It doesn't feel like work, it feels like fun, play, inspiration. When I work in this zone and it's flowing out of me, I can hardly believe people pay me to do this."

Actress and singer Debbie Reynolds has gone through a string of tough breaks, including three disastrous marriages, a recent bankruptcy, and a dwindling career. She has no choice these days. She has to work. "Sure, it's hard to do one-nighters and travel across the country," she admitted. "But my work is a joy, it's fun, it's my pulse, it's my life. I love it."

There were very few exceptions to this way of thinking. One of them, a security analyst, bluntly admitted that she hated her job but liked the income. "I thought about doing something I love, but I couldn't come up with anything that paid well. So I went for a job where I'd have enough money." Then she paused thoughtfully and added, almost as if it had occurred to her for the first time, "You know something? If I was passionate, I'd probably be making a lot more."

Most of the women I interviewed had much more optimistic expectations. They genuinely believed they could and would make good money in work they enjoyed. (They didn't necessarily expect to earn six figures, but they believed they'd do very well.) "I always wanted to be a teacher," Vivian Carpenter, a dynamic African American woman, told me. "I believe, no matter how impossible it seems, once you decide to do what you love and be excellent at it, the money will come. I walked in the highest-paid faculty person at Florida A&M University. I even made more than the dean who hired me."

Some women even took cuts in pay to pursue their passions. For example, seven years ago, Rikki Klieman was a big-ticket trial lawyer running her own Boston law firm. Today she's an anchor on Court TV, living in New York and making a fraction of what she once did. "I made a choice to halve my income and double my expenses," she said, explaining that at first she had to support herself living in two cities. "If I'd remained in the firm, I'd be making four times the money I'm making now."

Did she have any misgivings?

"None at all. Court TV is the perfect job for me," she declared, quickly adding, "Don't get me wrong. I want to make enough money so I don't worry. Financial independence is very important. I'm still getting six figures, enough to pay my bills and take vacations. But as my law partner said when I got the call to audition, 'This job has your name all over it. It's everything you've ever wanted.' And it is."

Not every six-figure woman is employed in the job of her dreams, but the vast majority found work that was fulfilling and stimulating.

Kris Evans is a freelance makeup artist for major motion pictures. She didn't follow her passion, which was acting, because, as she put it, "I didn't want to be a starving artist living on tuna fish."

Still, she affirmed, "I haven't entirely given up my dream. But in the meantime I'm loving what I do. It's a thrill seeing my work on the screen. I couldn't go to a job every single day that I hated. I couldn't do that no matter how much you paid me. I don't want my son thinking life is just making money."

Clearly it takes more than love to put food on the table or to hang your hat in the executive suite. Indeed, passion for work is just part of the equation, but, like logs to a fire, it's a very, very important part.

DO WHAT YOU FEAR

Focus and passion were vital, but something else played an even bigger role in reaching the six-figure sector. When I asked, as I always did, "What has been the most important factor in your financial success?" almost everyone responded, "Belief in myself" (even more than "hard work," "education," and "talent," the three runners-up). I absolutely expected these women to be supremely self-confident, and they were.

"You have to believe in yourself, that you can do anything you set your mind to," investment banker Celeste Chang said at the outset of our interview. That catchphrase—*I can do anything*—emerged as a recurring mantra throughout the interviews.

"I believe I can teach anything," corporate trainer Donalda Cormier told me. "That's how I got into this field. When I was in college, I walked up to a professor who owned a training program and said, 'I can teach that.' I had no track record, no experience. But I knew I was good at teaching. I continue to do this all the time. I'll see opportunities, walk up to people, and say, 'I can do that.' "

"Where do you get the nerve?" I asked.

"I have a lot of faith in myself," she replied. "In terms of my success, I'd rank belief in myself right at the top."

I figured that their confidence, their chutzpah, was the reason for their fabulous success. Well, it was and it wasn't. The real secret emerged, usually midway through our conversation, when I'd begin to notice tiny cracks in their confident veneer. This is where I learned that *belief in yourself doesn't mean the absence of self-doubt.*

Every woman admitted to grappling with feelings of inadequacy, incompetence, and fear. Fear of failure, fear of rejection, fear of criticism lay like fault lines just below the surface. But they looked and acted confident even when they didn't feel it. Abby, a corporate lawyer, may have said it best: "It's like being a duck. Calm and unruffled on the surface, but paddling like hell underneath."

Similarly, Donalda confided, "Even though I say I can do anything, when I'm in it, I go 'Oh shit, what have I done!' "

And even Celeste, with the self-possessed bravado typical of a young Harvard grad, told me, "Sometimes in a meeting people will be asking for my input, and I'll think, What do I know? Why are they asking me these questions?"

I was truly astonished to hear not only how many struggled with self-doubt but also how anxious they were others would find out. I'll never forget talking to an investment adviser who was a partner in a prestigious firm. A very high-profile woman in her midfifties, she was a well-known author, often quoted by the press and interviewed on television. I asked if she ever felt this way.

"Often," she said softly. "There are times I've sat in our board of directors meeting looking as if I'm reading a complicated report and

I don't know what the hell I'm looking at. But I put on a good show. I'm somehow able to pull it off."

I was amazed to hear this coming from such a poised, elegant, and accomplished woman. "I would never have guessed," I said to her.

"I know," she said, "no one would. I worry people will see I'm not that smart. A therapist told me it's called the Imposter Syndrome. I'm so afraid people will discover how dumb I am. I wrestle with this all the time."

So many of these dynamic women described wrestling with this very same devil. They felt they were a fake, that their success was a fluke, and their deepest fear was that people would see they're really a fraud. In fact, a number of women I contacted refused to be interviewed for that very reason. They genuinely felt they had nothing to offer and completely discounted their financial accomplishments. I suspect they were afraid I'd see through their ruse. Those whose success came quickly or who far surpassed all expectations were especially vulnerable to feeling like an imposter. There was a huge gap between how they saw themselves and how others regarded them.

Jenna Graham, who became the highest-ranking woman at one of the largest technology firms in the world, admitted to me, "I come from a blue-collar environment. The expectation in my family was that I would be a teacher or a nurse, never a corporate executive."

"How did you get beyond their expectations?" I asked.

"I don't think I have yet," she said, laughing. "There are times when I live looking over my shoulder, making sure I'm working hard enough, afraid someone will take it all away. I deal with it by doing more."

It wasn't just at work that she felt less than secure. After a big promotion, she remembers a friend saying to her, "You know, you

ought to get rid of that Chevy Malibu you drive. It's not really you."
That day Jenna decided to buy a new Mercedes. "But I was afraid to
even walk into the dealership, let alone buy that car. I was embarrassed. I went in thinking they'll know I don't belong here. They'll
throw me out. But they just said, 'Fine, the car will be ready in three
hours.' I couldn't believe it was so easy."

Some reference to the Imposter Syndrome ran through so many
of these women's stories. Beneath their confident exteriors lurked
layers of insecurity. Yet despite their qualms, these women, like
Jenna, managed to become incredibly successful, professionally and
financially. How did they do it? Their secret is this:

Feel the Fear. Have the Doubts. Go for It Anyway.

They bought the car, taught the course, translated complex mate-
rial, and they didn't let their fear stop them. What's more, some of
them actively sought out the kind of situations they feared most.

Miriam left her job at an art gallery, got an M.B.A., and took a
position in finance at a global investment firm. "I knew it was going
to be really hard and challenging," she told me. "I never in a zillion
years thought I'd be doing this. One of the reasons I am is to face my
demons, the things that scare me."

What were those demons? Her reply: "There is so much rejection when prospecting clients. That's why I took it. I wanted to overcome my fear of rejection. I saw what it did to my mother. It wasn't
rejection that held her back, it was her fear of it. I said, 'I'm not
going to do that.' "

How has it been to go from the art world to Wall Street? I asked.

"I feel like a fish out of water," she confided. "But I felt that way
at Harvard, too."

Feeling like a fish out of water was a common theme among aspiring women who made dramatic career changes into more lucrative (often male-dominated) fields. But the biggest challenge for nearly everyone was simply trying to stay afloat in a sea of endless obligations.

THE BALANCE BEAM

The whole notion of trying to achieve success on the job and enjoy a life outside of it is an ongoing struggle for practically every workingwoman. *USA Today* (March 30, 2000) described them as "whipsawed women . . . careening around like a pinball between work, home, errands, and carpools." But it's especially tricky for women in the demanding jobs that pay the highest wages.

It's no surprise that balancing work and personal life is the most mentioned, most taxing quandary these high earners encounter, particularly as they try to merge their desire for marriage and family with their aspirations for financial success. It is something men rarely have to deal with. "I've yet to hear a man ask for advice on how to combine marriage and a career," women's advocate Gloria Steinem once observed. But we hear it incessantly from women.

Katie Cotton, manager of corporate communications at Apple Computer, was young, single, and very hardworking. "Do I think I could have my job and balance a family?" she wondered out loud. "I really don't. I know there are women who do, I just don't know how the hell they do it."

She had ended an eleven-year relationship because of her resistance to marriage and having kids.

"I wouldn't be happy plopping out a baby, then leaving and working a sixty-hour week. I am concerned about even taking four months off for maternity leave." She paused, then added reflectively, "I do wonder if I'll get to age forty and regret not having kids. I'll have all this money, a great career, but will that be enough?"

The struggle for balance is even more apparent in the life of the single mom. When I first called to schedule an interview with Stephanie French, vice president of corporate contributions for Philip Morris Companies Inc., she was about to go into the hospital for surgery—and was actually looking forward to it. For her, this was a rare chance to rest, she said, explaining that normally she worked all day, rushed home to have dinner with her kids, then most nights left again by eight for a business function.

"For a single working mom, it's always a terrible balancing act. You're never at work enough and never with the kids enough. You've got to make hard choices about your time. Sometimes you have to skip being home because you have to be at a business event. And then you'll feel terrible that you're not with your kids. It's constant choices, and you never know if you're making the right ones."

When I asked about her social life, she laughed wryly. "Dating? Try to get a date with me, unless you want to eat with my kids."

Even with a husband at your side, mothering while working is still a herculean task. The day I interviewed banker Lucy Tomassi, her nanny had just given notice, and she was in a dither. Having been a single mom, I understood her panic all too well.

"Will you look for another nanny?" I asked. Her answer captured the working mother's catch-22: "You know, it seems like a nanosecond since my son was born, and now all of a sudden he's four. I feel like I'm letting some of the best years of my life pass by. I'm feeling the tug of wanting to spend more time with him."

"Will you quit?" I asked.

The question made her gasp. "The idea of completely stepping out of the workforce terrifies me," she said. "A huge part of who I am is tied up with my work and my success. If I gave up work altogether, I'd lose a huge part of myself, of what makes me tick. I find that very frightening to think about." She paused, then acknowledged it's also the money. "For years, I've made sure I had this comfort zone. I'd find it hard to rely on my husband to bring home the paycheck."

The work/family dilemma is an intricate web of complex issues—issues of identity, autonomy, and a maternal instinct that exerts a fiercer pull than the force of gravity. No one understands that better than executive Ruth Harenchar. Early in her career, she told me, "I had to pass up opportunities because I wouldn't travel. One of us had to stay with the kids." When her husband sold his business, however, he opted to quit working and be the one to stay home. That gave Ruth the freedom to focus on her work.

"It had taken me sixteen years to break a hundred thousand dollars. It took me less than five years to more than double my income. Having a husband at home made a tremendous difference." But at the same time, Ruth discovered freedom had a dark side. "It made me incredibly selfish. I got so into it I became just like those awful stereotypes of men, obsessed by work, ignoring my family. My kids missed me."

This revelation forced her to reevaluate. "I started pulling back. I don't work on weekends now. I don't care what happens. I hang out with the family or play with the dog. It's so easy to get focused on work because you get so much of your self-worth from the job, especially if you're successful. I see why men get so consumed with work."

Ruth has finally settled into a workable equilibrium. That seems to be what happens. Over time the majority of high-earning women established their own brand of precarious balance. They each found, usually through trial and error, viable solutions for preserving their mental health while managing their multiple roles. Those solutions came from taking a hard look at their personal priorities, what they cherished most in life, and then discerning between what they thought they should do and how they really wanted to live their lives.

"At first I thought I had to be out there all the time," said business owner Mary Helen Gillespie. "Then I realized it's not worth it. And, you know, when I started talking like this I made more money than I ever did in my whole life. It was when instead of being driven to make more, I started saying how I wanted to live my life."

Others found their own unique, creative, and practical ways to stay sane while achieving success. For example, Judith Wicks opened a restaurant in her house. "My kids ran around behind me trying to keep up," she said, laughing. Scientist Jane Porter deliberately "advanced very slowly to focus on family," while psychologist Ingrid gave up eating, sleeping, and a social life. "My kids were my social life," she chuckled. A few, like lawyer Virginia Harding, cut back to part-time, while others, like Elena, a CPA, continued full speed but set limits. "I don't take work home. I don't work on the weekends. When I'm home, I'm home." Still others worked in spurts, then took time off, or made a change to less demanding jobs.

Katie Cotton, whose relationship ended because of her commitment to work, called a year after our interview with some startling news. She had reconciled with her boyfriend, gotten married, and was pregnant with twins.

"I decided to do it all," she declared, explaining that she and her husband will equally share parenting responsibilities with a lot of help from others.

Occasionally, women whose children were grown spoke wistfully about lost time. Karen Hopkins, president of the Brooklyn Academy of Music, looking back with a great deal of candor, admitted, "I gave up my son's early years by going back to work when he was three months old. At the time I thought I wanted to."

Are you sorry? I asked.

She shrugged and shook her head no. "I've had a great life, a great career, and a great son. I've had the chance to meet all kinds of people in the field I love, so that's the trade-off."

Karen has summed up the secret to striking a balance in the modern-day work world:

Think in Terms of Trade-offs, Not Sacrifices,

to Find a Workable Equilibrium.

After nine years of full-time motherhood, Andi Bernstein is back to work now, part-time, at a cable network. Still she rarely travels and will leave work early to attend her kids' activities. "I don't see this as a sacrifice," she asserted. "Sacrifice puts a bad spin on it. It is just a choice. When I was single there wasn't that choice to be made. You know, if you're not careful, you can get overinvested in work."

This battle for balance, to not get overinvested in work but still do what it takes to advance, is ongoing for virtually every successful high earner.

NO ONE PROMISED US A ROSE GARDEN

There's another battle that may be even more painful than juggling too many hats: contending with gender bias and sexual harassment. Not all six-figure women have to confront these problems. For those who do, however, it can be the most frustrating and distressing challenge of all.

Discrimination has always been a workplace threat for aspiring women, and these days, the higher a woman climbs, the more acute this problem seems to become. When Jenna Graham began being promoted into six-figure positions, she was appalled at the treatment she received. Once, the corporate jet with the top guys in the company took off without her. "They forgot me. They left me in Chicago. My purse and my belongings were on the airplane," she said incredulously. But that was hardly the most offensive act. During meetings in his office, the division director would leave the door open when he went to pee, with her sitting in full view of the bathroom. And after her biggest promotion, the men openly and derisively referred to her as "kind of a CEO."

Jenna never said a word. "I didn't want to be labeled a whiner," she explained. However, she had a redeeming moment at a meeting when a black executive stood up and said, "You know, I equate work here to when you come home at night and you say to your wife, 'Honey, is everything OK?' and she says, 'Yes, yes, everything is OK.' But deep down you know in your heart something isn't right. Well, that's the feeling I have here. And what's not right about working here is that I always feel like an unwanted guest."

"I was so moved," Jenna recalled. "The women and minorities in the audience all knew what he was talking about."

Many, though surely not all, of the six-figure women I interviewed had themselves felt like an interloper. But the vast majority of them spoke of much more subtle slights. Corporate women complained of being excluded from social occasions, passed over for promotions, or ignored for tough assignments. Entrepreneurs resented not receiving the same referrals, networking opportunities, or start-up capital as their male colleagues.

"I wish we were all treated equally, but it just isn't the case," Mari, an investment banker, told me. "The guys will get asked by the people that run the firm to go golfing, but they won't ask me because I'm a woman. So my peers are hanging out with the decision makers on weekends and I'm not invited."

How do you handle that behavior? I asked her.

"I've grown to accept it." She sighed. "I don't like it, but what can I do? I counteract it by not messing up, not making mistakes, and working harder."

Mari's solution—recognition, not resignation—is how most high-earning women dealt with gender bias and other injustices. As Valerie Gerard, a senior executive of Cable & Wireless PLC, quoted her mentor on these kinds of difficult situations: "Just keep the blinders on and everything else will fall into place."

Hedge-fund manager Renee Haugerud put it this way: "The point is to accept the fact of it, get angry enough to do something about it, but not blame or become a victim. I had a female boss who said to me, 'Renee, you're right. It's unfair that these guys are getting allocated ten million dollars and you just got allocated one million dollars. But you're a good trader. Just put your head down, work harder than they do, and you'll make more money. That's just how it is.'"

Many six-figure women also find strength in a sense of humor. "You know what strikes me as really funny?" said Elena, a CPA. "After all these years, I have never received a referral from an attorney where the client wasn't a woman. Ninety percent of my clients are men, but somehow the lawyers don't think of me as a qualified professional adviser for their male clients. They refer the men to my partner Mark."

"I think that would bother me," I said.

"Not me. I just have to laugh."

Lawyer Tracy Preston told me the same thing. "If I internalized every time someone said something racist or sexist I wouldn't be able to function. There's always some incident that'll be jarring, but I recognize it's people's ignorance. How do I deal with it? As they say, being black in America isn't easy, so you have to have a sense of humor. Otherwise you'd go crazy."

"My sense of humor is a shock absorber," agreed Patricia Cloherty, a venture capitalist. She gave an example. "My two male partners would get calls from clients who wouldn't work with a woman. I really didn't care. I'd just walk in and laugh, 'Hey, you're left with the dregs, and here I am.'"

These six-figure women had figured out a key secret for dealing with prejudicial treatment without losing their temper, their footing, or their perspective:

Sometimes You Just Have to Shrug It Off

and Have a Good Laugh.

THE HAPPINESS FACTOR

One thing is for sure: There's plenty of stress in the six-figure lanes. Coping with multiple roles, a challenging workload, and their minority status is no piece of cake for Successful High Earners. Yet despite the ubiquitous pressures, I found another frequently repeated, and very surprising, theme. As a whole, six-figure women are a very happy bunch. Their conversations were liberally sprinkled with words like *gratitude, fortunate, lucky,* and *blessed.* It was incredibly heartwarming to hear how joyful and appreciative these women were.

"I live in a posture of gratitude," said Beth Chapman, a divorcée who once had to take in boarders to pay her mortgage. "I lived in a survival mode for so long. Now I have it all. I am amazed at the kind of life I've been able to sculpt out of my crazy past. I'm the most fortunate woman I know."

They seemed to be always counting their blessings. Rikki Klieman, the anchor from Court TV, told me, "Every night when I was a child, my mother would come in my bedroom and say, 'Rikki, what are you thankful for today?' She died years ago, but every single night I still tell her how thankful I am for my life. How happy I am."

Was the money the source of their happiness? To some extent, yes. Money unquestionably afforded these successful women opportunity, freedom, well-being, and largesse.

"It's not the money I love," business owner Tracey Scott explained. "But I love what the money makes possible, the way it's changed my life. The more money I make, the more I've been able to help my family. I've made sure my younger sister had money for a good education. I've made things much easier for my mother."

"Money is liberating," echoed venture capitalist Patricia Cloherty. "You know you can take care of any health problems. If a friend needs help, you're there. It gives you access in the political world, and you can help those without access to get it."

I remember a delightful point in my interview with African American business owner Claire Prymus, after she'd described how humble her upbringing had been and how deeply, profoundly wonderful her life was now. "After we finish this interview," she said, giggling, "I think I'm going to drive up to Napa, check into a good hotel, have a nice dinner. I have the financial freedom to do that. When I look at where I came from, I feel so blessed."

These women demonstrated an indispensable secret for living a prosperous life of genuine wealth:

Appreciate Abundance.

We might want to rethink that old saw that money can't buy happiness. In a recent NBC/*Wall Street Journal* poll, a third of those with six-figure incomes reported they were happy, while just one in five earning less than $30,000 felt that way (www. echonyc.com). "Wealth does correlate modestly with happiness," reports David Myers in his book *Pursuit of Happiness.* "[But a] better predictor of happiness is a person's satisfaction with his or her income." I found the same in my study, even with the women who knew they were paid less than their male peers. According to studies, the most highly compensated women receive less than 3 percent of what the best compensated men make. But instead of focusing on the disparity, or becoming disheartened by its implications, the women I spoke to recognized and appreciated that they were making more than most Americans, certainly more than most women, and in many cases, more than they had ever dreamed they would.

"Yes, I'd be making a lot more money as a man, no question," one woman told me. "Every once in a while I'll think about it, but I am not a depression-minded person. I'd rather be happy. And I am."

Which is not to say that these successful earners don't get down in the dumps or have attacks of negativity. They do, and I sometimes called them when they were smack in the middle of a really bad spell. Yet, what struck me when I followed up was how they had invariably bounced back. For example, three months after interviewing the sobbing woman, a direct marketing specialist, I called her again to see how she was faring. She laughed when she heard my voice.

"You talked to me on the worst day I was having in twenty years," she admitted. Obviously, she was back on her feet. I found that the Successful High Earners refuse to stay a victim or remain down in the dumps for very long. They don't go into denial or act under pretense, but they work very intently to find the place where they can be happy again.

Admittedly, my initial interviews took place during an unprecedented economic boom. However, we were well into a recession when I reconnected with many of them to fact-check their quotes. Some were no longer bringing in six figures. Others, while still in game, were making decidedly less. And a few had lost their jobs. Yet, without exception, each one remained upbeat and optimistic when she spoke of her future. "The trick is to be flexible," said an entrepreneur. "This is only temporary," an executive asserted when she spoke of her diminished bonus.

And even Jenna Graham, the former technology executive who is now a full-fledged entrepreneur, told me enthusiastically, "I've never been happier. I love being my own boss. I love the potential of making a zillion dollars out of nothing. I'm not there yet, but I will be." However, it wasn't just the work, or financial possibilities, that made her glow. For the first time, she had a sense of balance. "I've moved to Florida. I have a life. It's like everything is happening as it should be happening." Indeed, Jenna was now living the secrets of a Successful High Earner.

EIGHT SECRETS OF SIX-FIGURE WOMEN

As my interviews progressed, I saw how much these six-figure women shared in common. I also began to see that these commonalities could be condensed into a set of guiding principles that inspired their achievements, the secrets to their financial success.

SECRET 1

Financial Success Is Possible in Almost Any Field, and Lack of Education Doesn't Have to Hold You Back.

SECRET 2

Working Hard Doesn't Mean Working All the Time.

SECRET 3

Focus on Fulfilling Your Values Rather Than Financial Gain.

SECRET 4

Loving What You Do Is Much More Important Than What You Do.

SECRET 5

Feel the Fear. Have the Doubts. Go for It Anyway.

SECRET 6

Think in Terms of Trade-offs, Not Sacrifices, to Find a Workable Equilibrium.

SECRET 7

Sometimes You Just Have to Shrug It Off and Have a Good Laugh.

SECRET 8

Appreciate Abundance.

Taken separately, none of these secrets will put more zeros on your paycheck. But in combination with the appropriate strategies, they become a formula for financial and personal success.

Before we discover just how that formula works, however, let's meet the women on the other side of the fence . . . the underearners. They, too, have something important to teach us.

2

THE LOWDOWN ON LOW
EARNERS

I have enough money to last for the rest
of my life, unless I buy something.
—JACKIE MASON

She sat across the table, deftly tapping the calculator keys. I was shuffling some papers while she balanced my books. It was part of our monthly ritual. This particular day, I looked up absentmindedly and asked my bookkeeper, "Andrea, would you ever like to make six figures?"

She quickly raised her head. "Oh, yes," she exclaimed.

"Well, why don't you?" She certainly had the brains, energy, and talent to be very successful.

"I just don't want to work that hard."

I looked at her in disbelief. Here was a woman who taught early-morning aerobics, cut hair by day, waited tables at night, and in her spare time freelanced as a bookkeeper and took courses at a local college. She was putting in more hours than many of the women I interviewed. But in her mind, if she had to work this hard for so little, what would it take to earn more? She couldn't imagine. Nor was it something she even wanted to attempt. Andrea was your classic underearner.

THE PHENOMENON OF UNDEREARNING

Jerold Mundis, the author of the first book on the subject, *Earn What You Deserve*, defines underearning this way: *"to repeatedly gain less income than you need, or than would be beneficial, usually for no apparent reason and despite your desire to do otherwise."* Simply put, an underearner is anyone who earns below her potential. Andrea fits the profile perfectly. She works hard to succeed, yet barely makes enough to get by, even though she has the ability and ambition to do better. Underearners aren't all poorly paid, however. You can make decent money and still fall into this category. *What distinguishes an underearner is that she could bring in more, and genuinely wants to, but, for whatever reason, she doesn't.*

It's estimated that one out of every three workers is an underearner, most of them women. Yet, despite the fact that this condition is so widespread, it is rarely discussed, little understood, and often unrecognized. I find it quite curious, and distressing, that the wage gap—the disparity between what men and women make—captures so much attention, when the far more insidious problem is our own proclivity to settle for less.

I once saw a cartoon, a humorous take on this sober reality. A group of men in suits are gathered around a conference table, and one of them is speaking. The caption reads: "Gentlemen, we need to slash expenses in half, so we're replacing each of you with a woman."

What's *really* wrong with this picture isn't so much that the women will be offered half a salary, but that the men know we'll readily accept it. Women unwittingly collude with this prevailing inequity by settling for less on our own accord. As a friend of mine put it, "The glass ceiling at work is nothing compared to the lead ceiling in my head." These mental caps, our own self-defeating limitations, should be our first order of business. After all, *how can we ever expect to earn as much as a man if we can't even earn as much as we ourselves are capable of making?*

Underearning is not to be confused with voluntary simplicity, a conscious choice to live with less. Deliberately reducing our consumption along with our cash flow is a calculated move to a saner, more peaceful way of life. The lives of underearners are anything but sane and peaceful. They are often overworked and financially strapped. They commonly live paycheck to paycheck, habitually scrambling to cover expenses, forced to go without in order to live on less.

Nor is underearning logically calculated or freely chosen—though we may try to convince ourselves otherwise. There's a big difference between an underearner scraping to get by, drowning in debt, and someone who knowingly, voluntarily does what she loves, even if it pays less, because in some very deep way it nourishes her soul, but still affords her an adequate livelihood.

Living in scarcity is almost always an unconscious decision, often a replication of our family coding. "I grew up with clichés like 'Money doesn't grow on trees,' " one woman told me. "My mom saved tinfoil and reused it. I brought those patterns into adulthood. I didn't have regular medical exams, proper rain gear, decent clothes. It's been really hard to let go of the messages, 'There'll never be enough.' "

Instead of letting go of old messages, underearners unwittingly re-create them. Karen McCall, the founder of the Financial

Recovery Institute, calls underearning a financial disorder, a money-related emotional problem right up there with compulsive spending and chronic debting. "It is a condition of deprivation," Karen says. "You can't possibly be living a full life if you're not meeting your needs."

In fact, a recent survey by the American Association of Retired Persons (AARP) found that seven out of ten Americans have had to significantly alter their life due to lack of funds—postpone their education, forgo vacations, stay in miserable marriages, go to work instead of staying home with the kids. Deprivation isn't always about poverty, either. Interestingly enough, wealthy inheritors are often notorious underearners.

I have a longtime friend who shares a background similar to mine. Sandy always knew she'd inherit a sizable estate from her grandfather. "I didn't try nearly as hard as I could have because I knew I'd be taken care of," she once told me. "So I always made only just enough to get by." At age forty-eight, she had neither a feeling of accomplishment, a sense of security, nor an inkling as to what she really wanted to do with her life. "It's not been very fulfilling or empowering. It's not as if I'd personally earned it. And there's always this feeling someone will take it away. Somehow I won't be able to keep it. If the income stops, there's nothing I can do to make money. I wouldn't even know where to start."

I knew exactly what she was talking about. Raised in a wealthy family, married to a stockbroker, given a trust fund when I turned twenty-one, I never gave money a lot of thought. I always worked hard but never earned much, and it didn't matter. My father kept assuring me I'd never have to worry. But as Sandy revealed, in the back of many an inheritor's mind is the nagging fear: What if I lost it? How would I get it back?

In my case, that fear became fact. Immediately following my

divorce, I struggled in vain to recoup the losses from my ex-husband's speculative investments. Finally, I went to financial counselor Karen McCall for help. She was the first one to tell me I was an underearner.

"Wait a minute," I protested, "I'm a writer"—as if my profession precluded any chance of higher pay. Besides, I wasn't looking to make money. (I guess in some high-minded way, I didn't want economics to taint the purity of my journalistic integrity. But the truth was—as seen in hindsight—my father never thought women should work. In an unconscious attempt to win his approval, I figured if I didn't make money then it wasn't a *real* job.)

More important, I reasoned, I wouldn't need to worry about making more money if I could just figure out how to successfully invest what I had left. That was all true, Karen agreed, but she gently insisted that overcoming underearning was an important piece of financial recovery. As a recovered underearner, I can now say with total conviction, it's not only important, it's compulsory—for financial as well as mental health.

Deep down, from the moment I heard the word, I knew it applied. But I had the hardest time actually owning up to the fact that I was one. Typical of an underearner, I had become a master of justification and rationalization. I had all sorts of reasons why I couldn't/shouldn't/wouldn't make more money. They sounded good. They felt sincere. And I genuinely believed them.

But the more women I interviewed who were earning good money, especially those in my own profession, I began to see that my logical explanations were simply flimsy excuses. Try as I might, I could no longer justify my reasons for being the poorly paid writer. Nor did I want to. Not only had I shortchanged myself financially based on a myth I held as fact, but even worse, I had denied myself the satisfaction of seeing tangible rewards from personal achievement and the deep sense of security that you can only get from being genuinely self-reliant.

My experience was typical. Most underearners will deny they are one to their dying day. After all, it's not a particularly flattering label. But the real reason behind our denial is that we're afraid. An admission of truth makes us accountable to change.

"Fear of knowing," the psychologist Abraham Maslow once observed, "is very much a fear of doing." If we acknowledge that we're underearners, then we'll have to do something about it. The very thought can be unsettling. It's so much safer, easier, more comfortable to keep things the way they are.

Even when our situation becomes really dire, it's amazing how desperately we'll cling to self-deception. Harriett Simon Salinger was a psychologist who made $40,000 a year as a clinical social worker leading personal growth seminars. "I was very good at what I did," she said, "but I kept living at the edge." By the time Harriett was in her sixties, she had depleted her savings and racked up $75,000 in credit card debt.

"I was in total denial. I didn't even want to look at how little I was making. If I saw I couldn't make it, I didn't know what I'd do at my age. So I refused to see. I stayed asleep." But Harriett was abruptly awakened when she was forced to declare bankruptcy.

Waking up, becoming aware, owning our deficits and honoring our desires, is the first step toward financial independence and toward life as a six-figure woman. Denial keeps us stuck. Recognition sets us free. Ask Harriett. She was one of the six-figure women I interviewed for this book. It took her only two years to go from making peanuts to top dollar. (We'll learn how in later chapters.)

One of the most encouraging things I discovered in my interviews was how quickly life turned around for women like Harriett once they opened their eyes and elected to change. When I talked to her, she was living in a beautiful apartment high in the hills of San Francisco and running a thriving business as a personal and executive coach. At age sixty-seven, she was fully vested in a pension plan and expecting to retire in seven years. "This money lets me choose how I want to live and work," she told me. She had also discovered the secret that high pay doesn't require crazy hours. Harriett works thirty hours a week, and "never on Friday."

OUT OF DENIAL

I made another intriguing discovery in the course of my research, especially in my "Overcoming Underearning" workshops. I noticed that underearners actually had a lot in common with their more affluent peers. For one thing, they are both extremely hardworking.

"My job is so demanding. I have no time for a personal life," Liz told the group. "Teaching is like housework—you can never get everything done. I'm working all the time." She sounded just like some of the six-figure women I was interviewing. And so did Jennifer, an artist who admitted, "I'm a workaholic, an overachiever, a perfectionist. I have to be the best at everything I do and I'm sacrificing my health, my life, all kinds of things for work." At most, she made $12,000 last year.

The women who took my course were also unquestionably capable, talented, and educated. Many were quite ambitious. And all of them genuinely wanted to make money. So why didn't they? As I've come to learn, underearners have certain distinct characteristics that keep them in lower income brackets. The nine traits listed below account for how they view the world, their work, and especially themselves. But most of all, these attributes explain why they remain underpaid.

THE NINE TRAITS OF UNDEREARNING

1. Underearners have a high tolerance for low pay.

Underearners consistently accept low-paying jobs or jobs that pay less than they need, usually for the "freedom" it gives them. I remember a woman in one of my workshops who made her living doing menial jobs, like gardening, baby-sitting, and house painting. "I always thought that if I took a high-salary job, I'd be locked into long hours, I'd have to give up my freedom." Yet she was sitting there complaining, "I'm working nonstop. I'm always working. That's all I do."

High earners make darn sure they're well compensated for their time at work, but it rarely dawns on (or appeals to) an underearner to set her sights on a higher salary. Whereas high earners normally lean toward more lucrative fields or strive for the steeper end of the earning curve, an under-earner usually can't even imagine herself making a great deal of money.

I can't tell you how often I've heard, "It never occurred to me that I could earn more." I've said it myself. It's especially true for women of my generation, whose earlier options were pretty much limited to nursing, teaching, or typing. Even today, most women gravitate toward the pink-collar ghetto where meager wages are a way of life. More than half of all workingwomen land in traditionally female, low-paying positions, especially clerical and service jobs. Chances are they fall into those jobs without questioning their options or challenging the precedent, thereby falling victim to their own limited visions.

"There's a part of me that says I can only be a teacher,"

said Marge, who admitted she hasn't enjoyed teaching for more than a decade. "My parents were both teachers. I never felt I had any other choices. Now I don't know what else I can do other than type memos."

Jaimie also fell into her position as director of a retirement community, a job that pays little but demands a lot. "It became very comfortable very quickly. I guess I've gotten stalled here," she admitted. "But I'm getting really tired." She told me she often works seven days straight, twelve- to fourteen-hour days.

When I asked both women why they don't look for something else, Jaimie let fly a string of excuses: She just hired a new assistant and needed to train him; she wanted to oversee all the new programs she'd put into place. Someday, said the fifty-year-old . . . someday . . . Marge, the teacher, simply sighed, "I just don't want to have to go back to school or start at the bottom somewhere and struggle my way up."

Someone once said, "The eye sees only what the mind is prepared to comprehend." To a nail, the whole world is a hammer. To an underearner, the whole world is a limitation.

I immediately think of an interview with Gayla Kraetsch Hartsough, a former VISTA volunteer with a Ph.D. in learning disabilities and emotional disturbances, who after six years of teaching realized she had gotten the wrong degrees. She should have gotten a master's in business. But, unlike Marge, she found a job with a consulting firm that paid her $4,000 less because she wasn't an M.B.A. "I approached it by thinking, If it works out, great. If not, I can go back to teaching again, which I had always enjoyed." She never went back to the classroom, and after eight years in the corporate world successfully started her own consulting firm.

Or take Elena, now a CPA, who spent most of her career as a college librarian. "But it didn't pay," she says. "The most I made was sixteen thousand dollars. I loved being a librarian, but I couldn't buy a home and put my kids through college on $16K. I wasn't out to make six figures, but I had to find a field where I could make more. If you don't go where there's a potential to make money, it doesn't matter how hard you work."

Both Elena, who was driven by a keen desire to increase her income, and Gayla, who wanted to do what she loved, ended up six-figure women. But neither Marge, constrained by visions of worst-case scenarios, nor Jaimie, justified by all kinds of logical reasons, can fathom the possibility of doing any better.

2. Underearners underestimate their worth.

Women, in particular, have a tendency to undervalue themselves, which is precisely what keeps so many earning beneath their potential. In a series of well-documented studies at various universities, women consistently paid themselves significantly less than men for a laboratory task, regardless of their previous income. The reason, some psychologists say, is what they call "depressed entitlement effect."

According to a recent issue of the *American Psychological Association Monitor*, the effect refers to a minority group's tendency "to devalue itself compared to the society's elite group." This is how disadvantaged groups rationalize their low status. Women see advantages held by the privileged group (men), and no matter how unfair, simply consider the situation a given. That's just the way it is, they conclude. At work, this way of thinking becomes a self-fulfilling prophecy.

Women accept lower wages because they presume they must deserve less.

3. Underearners are willing to work for free.

Underearners regularly give away their time, knowledge, and skills for nothing. They'll work at no charge without thinking twice. Most of the time, it's so ingrained, they aren't even conscious they're doing it.

"There were years I was working so hard, hard as I'm working now, doing just as good a job as I am now, but I wasn't making anything," recalled financial adviser Victoria Collins about her days as a preschool teacher. "I couldn't figure out why. Now I see it was because I was doing stuff for free and wondering why I wasn't making any money."

Now, like her well-paid peers, Victoria would never allow that to happen. High earners are adamant about putting a price tag on their work. Not that they don't volunteer for worthy causes, but that's a separate matter from earning a living.

When I interviewed Joline Godfrey, she had just been asked to speak at a conference focused on girls and money. And she was frustrated. Joline is a six-figure woman who founded Independent Means, a company that offers financial programs and products for girls.

"This was a for-profit event," she said with exasperation. "But when I told them my speaking fee, they went into shock. 'What fee?' they said. 'We can't pay you a fee.' I told them I couldn't do it for nothing. It would go back to everything that I'm working to change. It's not right to ask women to have economic empowerment and not practice it themselves.

"I have to have my knowledge valued," Joline declared.

"When someone asks me to do it for free, I say, 'If I give away my time and expertise, it says those things aren't worth much. And I know that's not so.'" When she does speak pro bono, she told me, "those are choices I make, not obligations."

Unfortunately, women in general are notorious for volunteering their time, and society readily, eagerly, exploits those who are willing. This practice is not good for your pocketbook. It's even worse for your self-esteem.

I once asked a screenwriter friend who's always helping people polish their scripts why she never takes payment. She sighed deeply. "I guess I don't have the confidence to charge," she said, quickly adding, "but I feel lousy about myself always doing things for free." Continuing to give our time away creates a self-perpetuating downward spiral of diminishing self-worth.

4. Underearners are lousy negotiators.

Underearners are reluctant to ask for more, whether it's to increase their fees or to request a raise. For some, it actually never crosses their minds to ask. "I remember saying to a career counselor, 'Is it OK to think about how much I might be able to earn?'" one woman told me. "I thought you just found a job and took what they paid."

But more often, underearners hold back simply because they're too scared. "What if I raise my prices, and they laugh in my face," said Annie, a bookbinder. She was agonizing over her inability to make a living doing what she loved. She knew she was grossly undercharging for her work but felt she had no choice. "I don't have any formal training in this. Who do I think I am to ask for more?"

Sherry struggled with this same issue. Hoping to make more money, she quit teaching school and started a business editing technical materials. But she ended up earning even less than she did as a teacher. "Why aren't I making as much as the big boys?" she asked rhetorically. "Because asking for money has been so painful. I don't want to make people mad, so I undercharge."

I promise you, asking for more is no picnic for high earners, either. Even Joline admits it's not easy. "I had long discussions with friends," she said, referring to the recent invitation to speak. "Hearing myself talk it out with them gave me the courage to go back and say no. If *I* have a hard time saying I can't do this for free, I imagine how hard it must be for other women."

It's hard for most women in all income brackets to demand more. High earners might not like it (and they rarely do), but they do it. That's how these six-figure women got where they are. They do what they are afraid to do (the fifth secret).

5. *Underearners practice reverse snobbery.*

Most of us harbor all kinds of distorted perceptions about money. Underearners, however, tend to have a particularly negative attitude, especially toward the people who have it. Many will tell you they don't like the rich. And women are more biased than men. In an AARP survey of twenty-three hundred people over the age of eighteen, a full 40 percent of the women (versus 20 percent of the men) believe that people who have a lot of money are greedy, insensitive, and feel superior.

I saw this for myself. I'd ask participants in my workshops

on underearning to complete the statement: "People with money are _____." They'd inevitably end the sentence with pejorative adjectives like "unhappy," "selfish," or "stressed." When I gave that same sentence to high earners, their responses ran along the lines of "lucky," "just people," and "free." Yet some of these same successful women admitted they hadn't always thought kindly of the wealthy. Part of their own shift to higher earnings was changing their attitude regarding abundance.

"I grew up with very painful money memories," says Lois Carrier, a former choir director, now a successful financial adviser. "When I first began making real money, I really felt guilty. How can I make money and still love the poor? How can I make money and not become snobbish? I had a lot of attitudes toward people who had money."

Lois worked hard on herself to "change the thought patterns that made no sense to me." As I realized during my phone call with my agent (when I confronted my own negative stereotypes of successful women), until an underearner comes to terms with her prejudices, it's unlikely she'll ever be prosperous. "I'm sure money would change me," a writer friend once admitted. "I'd become less caring. I wouldn't work from the heart. I see too many people going from being ordinary authors to making gobs of money and suddenly they have their noses in the air and their families break up."

Similarly, an entrenched underearner openly admitted her prejudices toward the wealthy: "I'm drawn to people who get by with very little. They have greater joy and less encumbrances. They're so much happier. I saw it growing up, with my friends from wealthy families. All that money looks really good from the outside, but there isn't much freedom and playfulness." There was no way these women, with this attitude, would ever let themselves become financially successful.

In addition to their disdain for the well-heeled, underearners are often turned off by what they assume rich people must do for the money. As one told me, quite adamantly, "People with money are unhappy. I think you don't see any people of great wealth having a lot of fun. Why? Because it comes with too many strings."

Professor Andrew Hacker, of Queens College, explained it this way in *Modern Maturity* magazine: "Most of us just want enough to feel comfortable and secure. Would you take a million if it fell from the sky? Sure. Do you want to work seven days a week and think about money 24 hours a day? Probably not."

Just about every underearner I've met believes real wealth comes at too high a price. "I don't know that I want to jump through all the hoops," a nurse told me. "From what I observe, rich people spend all their time managing, planning, and obsessing. This doesn't appeal to me. There's nothing life-giving about this in my view."

The irony is that few people work harder or obsess more about money—or rather, the lack of it—than underearners do. As the artist Willem de Kooning once aptly remarked, "The trouble with being poor is that it takes up all your time."

6. Underearners believe in the nobility of poverty.

At the same time underearners are spurning the wealthy, they are singing their own praises for surviving on so little.

Many of them take great pride in barely eking out a living, as if it's more noble and respectable to be one of the poor. Not only are people with money bad, they think, but so is money itself. "I always had strong convictions that money was evil," a woman announced in one of my workshops. "We had a sick cat when I was about five, and my parents couldn't afford medicine, so we had to put him down. I was so outraged. Money stopped my cat's life. I didn't want anything to do with money from that day on."

Still, until that moment, she had never equated her sizable debt with her childhood decision. Yet virtually every under-earner is operating under unconscious assumptions, usually made early in life, that determine her relationship with money. Whether it's family messages, personal experience, or religious indoctrination, many underearners genuinely believe money is tainted, materialism is bad, and there's something virtuous about surviving on a shoestring. According to this line of reasoning, they are much better people for rejecting financial gain.

Poverty, however, holds no appeal to high earners, who genuinely enjoy what money affords them, including the opportunity to tithe to their church and help others less for-tunate. Among high earners who have been poor, none hold any desire to repeat the experience. "Poverty is not roman-tic," stated an entrepreneur who remembers desperately try-ing to find a doctor to treat her brother because her family had no medical insurance.

"Women think you have to make a choice to do good or have money," said Joline Godfrey. "I never understood that. Why do you have to make the choice?" She always wanted to be a social worker, she told me, but was also determined to make "significant income." She didn't see those goals as mutually exclusive. After college, she found a job in the social work department at Polaroid. "In 1977, I was probably the highest-paid social worker in the country," she said, laughing. "Everyone in my class thought I sold out, that social workers shouldn't be working in private industry."

That's not at all how Joline saw it. "I had impact. I made a difference. I did great social work inside that company," she asserted. "And I also had a condo in Harvard Square."

"Money is a tool. It depends on how you use it," said six-figure entrepreneur Vickie Sullivan. "You can enrich yourself to the detriment of others, or you can use it to make the world a better place. Do I have enough money? Yes. Do I want more? You bet. Wouldn't it be great to give fifty grand to Habitat for Humanity so they can build houses for people? That would be amazing."

7. Underearners are subtle self-saboteurs.

One of the most effective ways bright women manage to remain dirt-poor or, at best, scarcely solvent is by tripping themselves up. Underearners unwittingly throw banana peels in their own path in all sorts of ways, like applying for work they're not qualified for, creating problems with coworkers, procrastinating or leaving projects unfinished, hopping from one job to another, always stopping just short of reaching their goals. The common thread is their *propensity to be scattered, distracted, and unfocused*. And they'll repeat the pattern indefinitely until they *consciously* step back and realize what they're doing.

"Why am I an underearner when I'm so educated?" a woman in my group mused. As she continued to talk, some answers emerged. "My parents were alcoholics who argued constantly about money. I carried that into adulthood. I won't ask for a raise so my boss won't explode. I feel guilty if I get promoted, like I got something I was unworthy of. I come up with all kinds of reasons to stop from being successful."

Dana, a real estate agent, thought back to all the times she cut commissions or didn't return a call from a potential client. "I wondered, Why do I do this? Then I thought about my family and how I was raised. I realized all the women in my family, though they had college degrees and excellent skills, viewed their moneymaking as supplemental to their husbands'. I somehow saw my career as a low priority. But I know better than to view my career as a hobby. So how do I change my mental image?"

Dana had already taken an important step the moment she took responsibility for her behavior. Underearners, typically, are quick to blame someone else—the government, their upbringing, whatever—for their problems. As a rule, under-earners believe the world controls them. High earners know they control the world.

One successful professional told me, "You can't come from much more of an unsupportive background than mine. My mother thought I was worthless. So did my ex-husband. But I think success has to do more with what *we* believe and take responsibility for. Everything that happened to me is a choice I made. So when a woman is in a situation where she's not making what she needs, well, she's the one who agreed to do the job."

Just as underearners will seek out a scapegoat, they will also search for a savior. Marina Holiday earned her living as a masseuse and a translator. But her claim to fame was being a finalist on the TV show *Who Wants to Marry a Millionaire,* where the grand prize was a rich husband. "I don't see anything wrong with using everything I have—including my physical attributes—to empower myself," she boasted in a magazine interview. "The winner was supposed to marry this man, fall in love, and have this wonderful life." In true underearning (and self-sabotaging) style, her definition of empowerment is to marry Prince Charming.

8. Underearners are unequivocally codependent.

Underearners will sacrifice personal security and private dreams by putting other people's needs before their own. Their kids, spouse, job, church, and friends all take precedence over their own needs and priorities. There's a fine line between loyal employee or devoted wife and sacrificial lamb. Underearners haven't a clue where that line lies.

"Do I like my work?" one underearner responded incredulously when I asked the question. "I'm doing this to get my daughter through school. And my husband off my back. Period. Yeah, I feel trapped in a job with diminishing returns. I have stress-related stomach problems. But what can I do?"

Subjugating our needs for the sake of others inevitably leads to resentment, depression, burnout, and breakdown. I was very moved listening to Lois describe her highly stressful twelve-year career as a choir director. "There came a time when I was emotionally and spiritually bankrupt. I had given till there was nothing else to give. I wasn't getting any rest. I wasn't taking care of myself.

"One night I was watching an animal show on TV and there were a group of lions who had just brought down an elephant. The elephant was lying there totally helpless, and the lions were eating it alive. That's the way I felt. I felt like my church was eating me alive. My friends were eating me alive.

"I think women do that. We're the caretakers. But we have to learn to take care of ourselves first, and not feel guilty. I always felt guilty if I did anything for myself."

One of the toughest challenges for just about every workingwoman I know is finding ways to satisfy her aspirations without ignoring her obligations or slighting those she loves. Six-figure women approach this challenge not as an issue of selfishness, but as a matter of balance.

"For me," Lois said, "when I saw that animal show, I couldn't believe I was identifying with the fallen elephant. That's when I realized I will either die or start filling myself up, because no one was going to do it for me. All of the people I cared for were not going to give me what I needed. I had to learn to love myself and value myself first before I could give to others. I think that's the key. When a woman puts her needs first, then everything starts to fall into place, including the money."

9. Underearners live in financial chaos.

In a 1997 Phoenix Fiscal Fitness survey, over half of the women polled expressed concern about outliving their nest eggs and agreed with the statement "I worry a great deal about money." With good reason. A 1998 study by the National Center for Women and Retirement Research found that among women age thirty-five to fifty-five, one-half to two-thirds will be impoverished by age seventy.

This is a very frightening statistic, particularly for under-earners who are obviously most at risk. They are more likely to be in debt, have smaller savings, fewer (if any) investments, and little idea where their money goes. Underearners often go from crisis to crisis, constantly moving money from one account to another, borrowing from Peter to pay Paul, careening hopelessly toward financial disaster.

"I know the havoc not having money can have in your life," Harriett Simon Salinger said. She had started her unsuccessful seminar business by selling her home at a huge profit. "I didn't pay a lot of attention to money," she said. "I lived well. I traveled a lot. I overpaid my employees. I supplemented my income with principal. I kept throwing money into the business. I had no idea what I was doing. Filing for bankruptcy was the hardest thing I ever did. I had to start over at age sixty-five."

Clearly, high earners are not all the savviest financiers. Many I interviewed had virtually no interest in the subject. But with rare exception, they lived within their means and were fiscally responsible. If they had credit card debt, which very few did, it was negligible. They were conscious spenders and disciplined savers. Virtually every one regularly contributed to her retirement fund, usually the maximum allowed. They deliberately took the steps that spared them from the nagging weight of "not enough" that underearners typically experience.

"I don't like being poor," a woman who worked as a receptionist told me. "I don't like the fear of what's going to come in the mailbox, or when the phone rings, who's going to say, 'We have to close your account' or 'Your check just bounced.' I don't want to be one of those old ladies who has to be put in a state-run facility."

Underearners may not like being poor, but they're even more averse to being responsible. "I never balanced my checkbook," Dr. Gale Cave, a former underearner told me. "I never wanted to know what I had because I was afraid I didn't have enough." Underearners are experts at finding ways to avoid dealing with money—from not balancing their checkbooks to bartering for services.

Financial counselor Mikelann Valterra told me about a client who bartered for everything she possibly could, including dental work and legal fees. "I won't barter with her," vows Mikelann. "She came to me because she's tired of scrounging, being behind in her payments, and always stressed out. She doesn't open her mail, her bills are turning into collection notices, she's one disaster away from being wiped out."

Mikelann is describing everyday life for many underearners. As long as chaos reigns prosperity is virtually unattainable. Chronic debt delivers the coup de grâce of higher earnings. (See page 263 for tips on getting out of debt.)

"Debt is about giving your energy away," Mikelann told me. "It cuts off our options, giving the illusion there's enough because when the money runs out, you can just whip out a credit card and continue spending. You never have to confront head-on that you aren't making enough. Which is why people use debt. It keeps you from confronting your fear of success, making hard decisions about how to earn more, and experiencing the discomfort when life becomes more expansive."

In other words, getting out of debt takes a lot of courage. I've watched the women in my underearning groups actually break out into a sweat or go into panic when they went to make the final payment on their credit card. It was like "Now what?" Many were actually tempted to fill the void with the familiarity of financial chaos rather than choose the unfamiliar and untested path to financial success.

THE UNDEREARNER'S BIGGEST CHALLENGES: FINANCIAL INSECURITY AND REDUCED OPTIONS

The fact is, underearners set themselves up for a lifetime of increasing uncertainty and diminishing options, of greater risk and fewer safeguards. Poorly paid women have the most to lose by keeping themselves in the downward cycle of escalating poverty and debt.

Not only are we living longer, but there's a good chance at some point we'll be on our own, perhaps responsible for children and/or aging parents. Research tells us the average woman spends seventeen years caring for kids, eighteen years caring for parents. And in all likelihood, we'll have little support to fall back on. Most of our safety nets are gradually becoming an endangered species—the extended family, the neighborhood, religious organizations, Social Security, even marriage. If a woman has money in the stock market, chances are she started too late, put in too little, and invested too conservatively to accumulate enough to finance her retirement. Our ability to provide for ourselves is our best, and often our only, protection.

Like it or not, money affects virtually every area of your life. Lack of it leads to dependency and hardship. It can limit your access to health care and lifestyle choices. It can keep you in an unhappy marriage and an unsatisfying job. It perpetuates the cycle of poverty and debt, of discontent and chronic stress.

"Underearning grinds down our spirit and hopes," says the author Jerold Mundis. "It exhausts us. It sucks the joy and pleasure out of our days. We come to live in fear that we're going to run out of money, that we won't have enough for the rent, the mortgage, our own tuition or our children's; that we'll be caught in a squeeze, hauled into court, end up as a bag lady."

The way out of underearning is rarely by working harder. Chances are taking a second (or third) job, putting in overtime, or finding a scheme to get rich quick will wear you out before it will make you wealthy.

The challenge for most underearners, as it was for me, is to face the problem squarely . . . before you hit bottom. Start the process by asking yourself these questions: Am I stressed about money? Or am I at peace with money?

An honest response will give you your first clue as to whether underearning could be an issue. Or try taking the "Am I an Underearner?" quiz below. If you find you qualify, get ready to change your life.

You are about to learn the seven strategies that will turn you into a Successful High Earner.

QUIZ: AM I AN UNDEREARNER?

Circle the statements that apply to you. Do this quickly, without thinking too much about your response. Circle the ones that might apply even if you're not quite sure.

1. I often give away my services (volunteering, working more hours than actually paid).

2. It's so hard to ask for a raise (or raise fees) that I just don't do it.

3. I have negative feelings about money and/or wealthy people.

4. I am proud of my ability to make do with little.

5. Someone or something else (IRS, ex-husband) is responsible for my financial situation.

6. I find ways to avoid dealing with money (bartering).

7. I tend to sabotage myself at work (apply for jobs not qualified for or low-paying, stop short of reaching goals, change jobs a lot).

8. I work very, very hard (long hours, several jobs). Or I go into excess and then collapse.

9. I fill my free time with endless chores and tasks.

10. I am in debt, with little savings, and no idea where my money is going.

11. I have a family history of debt and/or underearning.

12. I am vague about my earnings (I overestimate or underestimate income; I see gross, not net).

13. I continually put others' needs before my own.

14. I am frequently in financial pain or stress.

15. Recognition and praise are more important to me than money.

16. I am confident in my ability to make money.

17. I always live below my means.

18. I love money and appreciate what it does for me.

19. I am very optimistic about my financial future.

20. I experience very little fear or insecurity around money.

21. I am determined to get paid what I am worth.

22. I am passionate about my work.

23. I have very supportive, nurturing relationships (including spouse).

24. I admire wealthy people.

25. I have little or no credit card debt.

26. I get myself in situations beyond my ability and then rise to them.

27. I am resilient and able to bounce back when I fail.

28. I am filled with gratitude for the success I've achieved.

29. I work very hard, but I know I don't have to do everything myself. I know how to delegate and set limits.

30. I am tenacious in achieving my goals.

Scoring: If you circled two or more of statements 1–15, you're probably earning less than your potential, despite your efforts and/or desire to make more. If you circled two or more of statements 16–30, you're likely in the upper-income brackets of your profession or industry. Are you ready to go even higher?

3

RAISING THE BAR

The trick is not to die waiting for prosperity to come.
—LEE IACOCCA

One of my biggest surprises in interviewing six-figure women was hearing how many were once underearners. I talked to a previously destitute dancer; a former meter maid; a battered housewife with no education; plenty of ex-nurses, teachers, and secretaries; even past welfare recipients. These women, who were at one time barely able to stay afloat, are now riding the crest of the wave. I could almost picture them giving one another high fives for their financial feats. They became, for me, living proof of what's actually possible. In their stories I found inspiration and infinite hope. Their message came across loud and clear: *Underearning need not be a life sentence.* We all have it in us to upgrade our status on the income scale. What I was eager to know, of course, was how did they do it? How can we?

CHANGE BEGINS WITH A CHALLENGE

When I examined the stories from former underearners, I made an interesting discovery. Their financial achievement was always preceded by a financial challenge. More specifically, the shift to higher earnings began as soon as they were willing to admit something was wrong. Each one told me how she had come face-to-face with a looming problem—some looming larger than others. I heard tales of bankruptcy or burnout, of feeling undervalued or overworked, of getting a divorce or desperately wanting one. Whatever challenge life had thrown at these women, no matter how subtle, how small, or how sizable and scary, it was their willingness to confront the problem head-on that gave them the impetus to change and propelled them, often very quickly, into the six-figure zone.

"Sometimes I think we have to be pushed," said an entrepreneur who told me how devastated she was when she discovered her former boss had tried to cheat her out of thousands of dollars in commissions and how scared she was to confront him. Yet that very incident pushed her into a six-figure venture. "I never would have gone off on my own if my last boss hadn't ripped me off like he did."

Most of us wouldn't budge, either, without a kick in the pants. The truth is, all problems—from a gnawing sense you could be making more to the gut-wrenching pain of staggering debt—have a purpose. They're there to get your attention. Financial challenges can be powerful catalysts, providing the critical opportunity to craft the life of your dreams. The key is to tackle your troubles early enough, while they're still only mildly disturbing.

As one high earner put it, "Pain forces action, but I'm trying not to let the pain get to where it's debilitating, to recognize it early enough and take corrective action." Otherwise, a problem ignored is a knife caught by the blade. You're holding the potential for heartache.

Most chronic underearners find themselves in this position. They either refuse to acknowledge their predicament or passively accept their fate. Thus, their incomes remain low, their troubles intensify, and their lives are defined by mediocrity or mayhem. But the ones who recognize something is wrong and decide to take action have very different outcomes.

"There is no such thing as a próblem," the author Richard Bach assures us, "without a gift for you in its hand." I fervently believe that whatever challenges we face are, in truth, our Higher Power, our inner wisdom—whatever you wish to call this inexplicable guiding force in our lives—knocking at our door with a gift in hand. Those first knocks are usually so gentle, however, that we often fail to notice. The restive stirrings of our heart are like the fine print in a contract, easy but unwise to overlook. Ignoring that job you don't like, the bills piling up, the checkbook that's never balanced is exactly what gets us into trouble. The knocks will grow louder, the challenges more difficult, the pain more intense, until we finally open our eyes and respond.

Years ago I found this quotation, which I've hung on my wall: "We turn to God for help when our foundations are shaking only to learn it is God who is shaking them." I would never have written my last book or pursued a career in financial education if my first husband hadn't plundered my trust fund.

Once we realize our challenges are purposeful, they need no longer be painful. Once we stop seeing them as stumbling blocks, we can start using them as stepping-stones. Indeed, the moment we stop waiting and start acting, we have the opportunity to walk through a doorway to a richer, fuller, more abundant life.

Remember Harriett Simon Salinger, who went from a struggling seminar leader to a six-figure woman in just two years? When I asked her how she pulled off such an amazing feat, she said, "My consciousness began to shift and all of a sudden, my earnings went up." Easy as that sounds, Harriett will tell you that the hardest thing of all is to bring the dark to light, to look truth square in the face. Harriett first had to admit she had a problem, which was not something she relished. "I didn't want to know how little I was making," she said. By the time she came out of denial, her finances had spun out of control. But even then, it wasn't too late. It never is. When Harriett finally sought help from a financial counselor, her life took a definite turn. As she became more self-aware, she started doing things differently almost by default. "I got smarter about running a business," she said. She got smarter not by going to school but by changing her thinking. There's nothing magic about this. It's a universal law: Our state of mind shapes our way of life.

Our state of mind, however, often resembles a rearview mirror. We head toward the future seeing only the images from our past, and then wonder why nothing ever changes. I once heard insanity defined as doing the same thing over and over and expecting it to be different. Given that definition, I can safely say underearning is a form of financial insanity.

The question is—how do we change that?

THE TWO-PRONGED PATH

Countless research studies, a host of experts, and all sorts of women's groups would have us believe that the only way we'll ever close the wage gap is if we get the right education (an M.B.A.), hobnob with the right people (male decision makers), go for the right positions (high-profile, revenue-generating jobs), or find work with the right companies (our own).

While all these are valid suggestions, not one former underearner pointed to any of those things as the primary reason for her surge in salary. That's because upping our earnings is an evolutionary process. These standard prescriptions focus entirely on what I call the *outer work of wealth*, or the things you need to do—the practical tactics and specific behaviors—to achieve success. But as I've come to see, an exclusively external focus can be at best insufficient and frequently counterproductive.

So often, the actual problem isn't really "out there" but lies deep within us. So often, we've been subtly, almost imperceptibly, and unconsciously undermining ourselves all along. Therefore, instead of relying on solutions *solely* outside of ourselves, we'd get quicker results if we included self-exploration. The *inner work of wealth* means identifying and overcoming those internal barriers that trip us up. If there's one thing I've learned about life, it is this: *Nothing changes until we do.*

I saw how this works when I interviewed savvy investors for my first book. Like myself, some of them had for years struggled in vain to take charge of their money. It wasn't until they started addressing their personal issues that they finally achieved financial proficiency. In other words, at the same time they were learning factual information, the outer work, they were also doing the inner work, examining their thoughts, feelings, attitudes, and beliefs. It was the combination that enabled them to capably and confidently begin managing their money.

That same two-pronged process applies to making money as well, doing the work from the inside out. As Einstein once noted, "Our problems can not be solved at the same level of thinking we were at when we created them."

If you have any hope of raising the earnings bar, the place to start is with what's in your head. That's really the only thing you have any control over anyway. You can't eliminate cultural barriers, but you can certainly reduce your internal ones. You may not be able to alter your circumstances, but you can always change the attitudes you have about them. Never underestimate the power of your thoughts to create your reality. The mind is the most powerful tool you have for transforming your relationship to money and your ability to earn it. As Buddha observed, "All that we are arises from our thoughts."

I'll never forget a woman in my underearning group saying, "I buy lottery tickets with the firm belief I can win. But there's a strong part of me that can't imagine this kind of financial success." Is it any wonder she makes so little money with that kind of thinking?

It became so apparent during my interviews that high earners think differently than their lower-paid cohorts. Susan Bishop, an executive recruiter who works with only six-figure clients, told me as much. "When I deal with women who are not there yet, I see a very obvious difference. It's almost like I'm dealing in a different world. Those in the higher brackets think differently." In other words, these women operate on different assumptions, worlds apart from the nine traits discussed in the previous chapter that describe the mind-set of the underearner. Consequently, they make different choices, and those choices are directly responsible for the amount of money they eventually earn.

Bank executive Teri Cavanagh would heartily agree. "Once I had no sense of self-worth. It was in the tubes," she admitted. What changed? I asked. "Nothing changed but my thinking," she declared. "I made a decision to change my attitude and everything changed. I started visualizing myself making money, seeing my worth, making affirmations. I even took my checkbook and wrote hundred-thousand-dollar checks to me. I could see myself gaining confidence."

BEGINNING THE INNER WORK

The inner work doesn't require intensive therapy. But it does take some internal reflection, ferreting out the beliefs and attitudes about money that were forged at an early age by family patterns and cultural precedents. What we observe growing up sticks with us forever. Perhaps we saw our parents living paycheck to paycheck; our mothers employed in menial jobs, if working at all; our fathers bringing home the bacon or racking up debt; our families fighting about money or not discussing it at all; our ministers warning against "filthy lucre"; our storybooks promising our prince will come and our magazines advising us how to trap him when he does—whatever the particular scenario was for each of us growing up. All the while, we're watching, listening, absorbing, and unconsciously deciding how we will relate to money in our lives. These initial images are installed like software in our brains. Our psyches become programmed. Our actions go on autopilot.

Every underearner in my group eventually came to the same conclusion. "I've had all these bedrock ideas that I've never consciously realized but have been acting on," one of them declared. "I mean, I hear myself saying things like 'It's not OK to have money without struggle' or 'People with money are unhappy.' These notions are contradictory, juvenile, and not useful, but I've been basing my life on them."

Over the course of our lives, most of us have been mindlessly making choices based on unconscious beliefs that have no basis at all in reality. Then we wonder why life isn't shaping up in the way that we'd hoped, despite our best efforts. The challenge is to bring these beliefs into awareness so you can consciously decide if they are serving you or sabotaging you. As you understand what's been getting in your way, you can begin making new decisions, taking different actions, ones that will steer you toward higher earnings. You will find opportunities to do this inner work, along with the outer work, woven into each chapter throughout the book. Also, at the conclusion of this chapter are a series of exercises I give to my groups. These exercises, based on the work of financial recovery expert Karen McCall, have helped scores of people examine their beliefs and attitudes, thoughts and feelings, choices and decisions around money.

You, too, may find that your way of thinking has prevented you from developing the traits that characterize a six-figure woman.

SIX-FIGURE TRAITS

When I studied the transcripts of my interviews with high earners, searching for the common traits, I realized that every single woman in my study had four attributes that her lower-paid peers visibly lacked. I have come to see that these four traits are absolutely essential if a woman is going to effectively and permanently change financial lanes. I call these four mandatory traits the Must-Haves.

1. *A profit motive.* Money per se may not be their driving force, but six-figure women absolutely expect to be well compensated for their work. They *want* to make money. They feel good about making money. They enjoy what money gives them. Profit, to these women, has a positive ring.

2. *Audacity.* Every woman I interviewed came to a point where

she had to step outside her comfort zone and do something she wasn't completely sure she could do. It was rarely an experience she relished, nor did she always succeed. But she worked up the moxie to make the effort.

3. *Resilience.* They all had the grit to get back up and keep going when they didn't succeed or when they encountered setbacks.

4. *Encouragement.* Six-figure women have tremendously nurturing relationships with one or more people who believe in them, support them, continually root for them, and sometimes prod them along. Some, but definitely not all, had encouraging parents. Every one has remarkable friendships. And for those in a committed relationship, a supportive husband or partner is invariably cited as essential to their success.

In addition to these Must-Haves, there are three qualities that are extremely beneficial for financial success, although not obligatory. Most, but not all, the women I interviewed possessed each of them to some degree. The extent to which they did, however, made financial success easier to obtain and more enjoyable. I call these three the Big Helpers.

1. *Self-awareness.* They strive to know who they are and what they want—their goals, values, priorities, skills, and talents.

2. *Nonattachment.* They are willing to let go of what doesn't work or holds them back.

3. *Financial know-how.* The most successful women understand and follow the rules of money.

Anyone who can read this book has access to all seven traits. You don't have to take out a student loan or become a slave to the system.

The only requirement is a desire to change and the determination to do so. The women I interviewed will show you how to establish a profit motive, gather encouragement, acquire self-awareness, learn about finances, and practice audacity, nonattachment, and resilience. They will show you how to foster and fortify each trait by doing the inner work along with the outer work. In the following pages, you'll learn detailed, specific strategies for putting these traits into practice.

You can either wait for a catastrophe to force you into action or heed those subtle stirrings to start the ball rolling. I strongly recommend the latter.

W A R N I N G !   W A R N I N G !

Be forewarned. Anytime you do something new that runs counter to your prior conditioning, your habitual brain immediately protests: "Watch out, this doesn't feel right! Stop immediately." Peter Senge, in his brilliant book *The Fifth Discipline*, calls this reaction "creative tension." Tension, explains Senge, is produced when our aspirations are at odds with our early impressions or our understanding of reality. This tension feels terrible, but it has a purpose. It forces us to act.

That's because humans hate tension. We'll do anything to reduce it. One way to do that is to lower our sights, give up the goal, and sink back into old patterns. This is the quick and easy fix most underearners take. A tougher, more uncomfortable solution is to stick to your decision and use those tensions as a driving force that pressures you to keep moving forward.

This takes guts, no question about it. The closer you get to achieving your goal, warns Senge, the stronger the forces pulling you away become, the louder your brain protests, and the more urgently you want to revert to old patterns. I've seen it repeatedly in my groups for underearners. They'd fall apart at the brink of success. They'd get cold feet, feel guilty, doubt their abilities, recall the pain of old failures, worry they made the wrong decision. My advice was always the same. It's OK to feel bad. Just don't let it stop you.

Here's the biggest secret to overcoming your past and upping your earnings: *You've got to be willing to be uncomfortable.* For us pleasure-seeking, pain-avoiding creatures, that's a very tall order. It's certainly not comfortable to face up to a challenge or to acknowledge a problem, and it's especially unnerving to eschew our habitual ways of handling them. Yet, that's exactly what's required.

The real work in raising the bar is to stop doing the same old thing you've always done, to try out new strategies, to ignore false alarms, to resist the urge to quit, and to refuse to fall back into familiar terrain. The ability to tolerate discomfort—doing what might not feel good, but doing it anyway—is the only way you'll ever complete the path to financial success. It helps to keep in mind that *the discomfort is temporary, but the payoff is extraordinary.*

I remember a very sophisticated businesswoman telling me about her impoverished background and her early efforts to support herself. "I never related to being an underearner. Now I see I earned way below my capacity for years. The first time I said I wanted to earn eighty thousand dollars I about passed out afterward. It didn't feel real. I could hear my mother saying, 'Who do you think you are?'"

At the time, she was making $23,000 in sales. When she told people her goal, they looked at her as if she was crazy. She suspected they were right. "I felt so much shame, like it was too grandiose," she recalled. But over the next three years, she slowly, steadily increased her earnings, though they were still nowhere near her target.

"Then one day," she recalled, "I was walking on the beach and it hit me—I could make a lot of money in my business. I just needed to do some things differently. It felt awkward to even think that, but a part of me knew I had what it took to go to the next level." That was the year she crossed into six figures.

THE THIRD PRONG

The real payoff, as many have discovered, is far more about personal enrichment than financial remuneration. As you aspire to monetary success, expect to find yourself simultaneously drawn to search for deeper meaning, to want to fulfill a larger purpose, and to have far broader impact than you ever anticipated. "It's time to start living the life we've imagined," writer Henry James chides us. It was as if the women I interviewed had heard those words and were taking them to heart. I call this the *higher work of wealth*.

"The money is secondary," Michele Page, a six-figure graphic artist, told me. "That the universe has given me challenges I've been able to meet so I can know my potential, that's the best thing I've gotten out of all this. Though it's wonderful to know I can take care of myself and my family, there isn't a better feeling in the world than knowing I can go out and be an active participant in the world, actually make things happen, and help others achieve their dreams."

Traveling the path to financial success imbues you with the confidence, competence, and resources to make a genuine difference in the world, to achieve your dreams and help others achieve theirs. This is the gift your financial challenges have in hand for you.

The key: Don't wait until you "feel like it" to start, and never give up because it "doesn't feel right." "Embrace what does not come naturally," Swami Chetananda admonishes us. "Only then will you stop limiting yourself and allow the deepest part of you to express itself in ways you may not have imagined just yet." This is the discipline of financial success and the incentive for achieving it.

PAVING THE WAY–POINTS TO PONDER

Before we continue, let's do a bit of inner work in preparation for what lies ahead. I'd like you to turn your attention inward and allow any unconscious assumptions you have about money to rise to the surface. Hidden beliefs will eternally hold you hostage. It's awfully tough, if not nearly impossible, to break free from an unseen enemy. The following questions are designed to help you identify those hostage holders. Once you see them, you can start to change them. Sometimes, clarity itself brings closure. Take a moment to think about each question; observe your immediate response (it may not be your final answer). As you proceed through these pages, hold these questions in mind. Better yet, keep a journal as you read, beginning with your answers to these questions. Often, the most profound insights emerge gradually.

Ask yourself:

1. Do I *really, really* want to earn more? Why?
2. If I don't, what's that about?
3. Do I believe I *can* increase what I make?
4. Is there a part of me that doubts my capacity to change?
5. How would my life be different if I had more money?

The more honest you are with yourself, the more helpful your insights will be.

If you're ready, let's open the door and step over the threshold, to enter a world full of possibilities. It's time to start traveling the path to a life richer in more ways than you might ever have dreamed. To this end, we will turn our attention to the seven strategies and learn how to turn each of the six-figure traits into a specific, viable tactic for upping your earnings.

JOURNAL EXERCISE

Write out your responses to the following questions.

1. What is your earliest memory of money?
2. Were you given an allowance growing up? Were you paid for chores or grades? What was your experience being paid (or not being paid)?
3. How old were you when you first started to earn money? What did you do? How did you feel? What's the most you've ever made? The least?
4. How was money handled in your family? What messages were you given about work and money? What was your mother like with money? Your father? Was there any emotional trauma around money?
5. What was your biggest fear about money when you were younger? Your parents' fears? What is your greatest fear now?

Source: This exercise is adapted from It's Your Money: Achieving Financial Well-Being *by Karen McCall (Chronicle Books, 2000).*

A MEDITATION:
THE EARNING-CEILING EXERCISE

Close your eyes and picture yourself earning the amount specified in each statement. Really take it in as if you are truly earning this amount. Be aware of how you're feeling and thinking at each level.

Then write down your reactions. Where was your ceiling, the point at which you couldn't imagine making any more?

1. Imagine you are earning $5,000 a year. How do you feel? What are your thoughts?
2. Imagine you are earning $10,000 a year. How do you feel? What are your thoughts?
3. Imagine you are earning $25,000 a year. How do you feel? What are your thoughts?
4. Imagine you are earning $50,000 a year. How do you feel? What are your thoughts?
5. Imagine you are earning $75,000 a year. How do you feel? What are your thoughts?
6. Imagine you are earning $100,000 a year. How do you feel? What are your thoughts?
7. Imagine you are earning $250,000 a year. How do you feel? What are your thoughts?

Source: This exercise was developed by Karen McCall.

THE DECISION-MAKING PROCESS

After you read each question, close your eyes and imagine that you're talking to different parts of yourself. For the first three questions, talk to yourself as you are now. Then imagine yourself having a conversation with you as a child (really picture yourself as a youngster, say five to ten years old), a teenager (see yourself about thirteen or so), and with

your negative ego (which often looks like a critical parent). Finally,
come back to yourself, as you are, after having these dialogues. Write
down whatever these different parts have to say. Observe how you feel as
you respond to the last question. If you have any resistance, repeat the
exercise.

1. How much do I want to make?
2. Why do I want to make that?
3. Why don't I want to make that?
4. What does my child say?
5. What does my adolescent say?
6. What does my negative ego say?
7. Why will I let myself make that amount?

4

STRATEGY #1:
THE DECLARATION
OF INTENTION

intention (n): a determination to act in a certain way
—MERRIAM WEBSTER'S COLLEGIATE DICTIONARY

"How does one become a butterfly?" she asked pensively.
"You must want to fly so much that you are willing
to give up being a caterpillar."
—TRINA PAULUS

"Was it your goal to make a lot of money?" I asked Ruth, a highly paid computer expert. This was always one of my first questions to interviewees, and I was beginning to notice a pattern in the responses I was getting.

"No, I have to admit, it wasn't," she replied. "It was the recognition that motivated me. But *somewhere* in there was the intention to make good money."

"You had the *intention* to make more money?" I asked, belaboring the word that had jumped out at me.

"That's true," she replied. "I was thirty years old, a poverty-stricken professional dancer. I was tired of being poor. So I made a decision. I said, 'OK, Ruth, it's time to actually make money.'"

There it was. The declaration of intention. I'd heard it in virtually every interview I'd done, though often cloaked in different words. Each woman would describe that point in her life when she said to herself, "It's time to make some money." And, in an almost uncanny way, the instant she made that explicit declaration to make more money her life took a definite turn.

When you recognize the power of the profit motive, you take your first major step toward financial success. It's the point of entry to higher earnings, the first strategy for becoming a six-figure woman. Indeed, not one of us will achieve financial success unless we make up our minds that's what we want.

THE DECLARATION AS DESTINATION

Many women I interviewed made the declaration early in life, while very young or still in college. "When I was a kid, I only had hand-me-downs," said a senior executive. "I always knew I'd make plenty of money so I'd never have to do that again."

Others came to it much later, sometimes under duress because of divorce, death, financial devastation, or just out of sheer frustration. "When I saw my husband wasn't going to make it," an American Express executive recalled, "I said, 'God damn it, it's up to me, and I'm going to do it.'"

A few of the women I interviewed always just assumed they'd make top dollar. Some simply started making money, liked the way it felt, and wanted more. Still others watched their colleagues, often men, drawing high salaries and figured, "If they can do it, why can't I?"

"The shift occurred for me when I began working for a firm with three male partners," explained Victoria Collins, a teacher turned financial adviser. "For the first time I was around people who had a profit motive, who valued their services appropriately. Understanding the profit motive was the key for me."

It was the key for every six-figure female I interviewed. Whatever these women did, they did it with the stated intent to earn a good living. They didn't necessarily aspire to a specific amount, nor was money their primary goal. But they were unquestionably motivated to make a profit. As one woman said, "Money was not the major thing, but it was definitely a destination, someplace I wanted to end up."

It may seem a contradiction, a paradox of sorts, that these women vehemently denied money was their goal, yet in the very next breath plainly said they were out to make money. In their minds, however, the two statements were not mutually exclusive but intrinsically linked. Each woman in search of her dreams knew that it would take dollars to make her dreams possible. As entrepreneur Claire Prymus put it, "I wanted to be self-sufficient, get out of debt, own property, be a success. I strove to make six figures and I did it. Now I'm looking at seven figures."

OPEN TO THE POSSIBILITY

I discovered an important secret about this strategy: Certainty, or lack of it, is inconsequential. You need only be open and receptive to the possibility, not necessarily completely convinced you can do it. So many of these high earners, when the thought of big money first crossed their minds, never really believed it would actually happen. Author and consultant Karen Page, for instance, decided in college she'd one day make $100,000. "It was the most outrageous number I could think of. It didn't seem doable," she said. But by age twenty-seven, she was making that much.

Nor did they know precisely how they would achieve all those zeros. In fact, most hadn't the vaguest idea. "I knew I was going to do it, I just didn't know how," Dr. Gail Cave said of her determination to make enough money to leave her abusive husband, even though she had no skills, no work experience, and no education. Through sheer grit, she became a successful dentist who makes a fabulous income working part-time.

One of the most hopeful messages I learned from these six-figure women is that we need not fully believe something is possible, much less have a full-blown plan firmly in place. We just have to decide what we want and be willing to do whatever comes next. Buoyed by this insight, I took a Post-It note at the beginning of this project, wrote down $125,000, and stuck it on my computer. That was my earnings goal for the year. How was I going to do it? I hadn't the slightest idea, especially since I'd never earned anywhere even close to that in my entire life. But in the words of Martin Luther King Jr., "You don't have to see the whole staircase. Just take the first step in faith."

When you commit to a goal without knowing exactly how you'll achieve it, you automatically trigger a tremendous power. When your intention is strong and your commitment is staunch, the how-tos invariably show up. I saw over and over how once the women I was talking to set their sights on higher earnings, lo and behold, that's what they got.

INTENTION ATTRACTS SUCCESS

Some attributed their success to a matter of luck. But, as I observed, luck is a frequent companion of a firmly fixed focus. It's almost as if our intentions become magnets, inexplicably drawing to us whatever we need to take the next step. "Inherent in every intention is the mechanics for its fulfillment," says Deepak Chopra. The women I interviewed regularly spoke of the synchronicities they encountered on the path to success.

"Once last January my income was down," Harriett Simon Salinger told me of her executive coaching business. "I immediately said I wanted eight new clients. By January twenty-second, I had eight. I stated it and they showed up. Whenever I get scared, I just breathe and trust in the strength of my intentions."

Similarly, when choir director Lois Carrier finally decided to quit her job in the church, she was amazed at the coincidences that occurred. "When I made the decision to change the way I was living," she said, "God just sent people into my life who were more enlightened than me, who talked to me, who helped me, who really made a difference." One of those enlightened people was a financial planner. "I got enormously excited about what he did for people. I was just raving about how fabulous it was," she recalled of her visit with him. He responded by urging Lois to do it, too. Her reaction was vehement. "I said, 'No way. I'm not going back to school.' He just kept after me for five months. Finally, I went to work with him. The rest is history." This former choir director now has a thriving practice as a financial planner.

Strong intentions have been known to produce sheer miracles. And for many of the women I interviewed, like Harriett and Lois, making a lot of money was truly nothing short of miraculous. But their success had less to do with providence than persistence. Their strong intent carried them through the toughest of times.

When your intentions are deep and compelling, and your commitment strong and inflexible, you're more likely to keep going when the going gets rough. When people tell you you're crazy or out of your league, when your accountant sees red and your future looks black, when what you want and what you've got are light-years apart, a clear intention is like a firm but gentle hand against your back and a voice that whispers, "Keep going."

"There are always setbacks in business," said Sheila Brooks, who spoke of the difficulties she had when she started her television and video production company a decade ago. "I was working long hours. The contracts weren't coming in. I didn't pay myself a salary during the first year. What kept me going was my belief that if I kept my eye on the prize and didn't quit, whatever the odds were, whatever the obstacles were, I could achieve whatever I wanted."

Sheila was right. And it was her intention to succeed that drove her into the arms of success. "Where your intention goes," Gary Zukav writes in his bestselling book *The Seat of the Soul*, "so goes you. Your intention becomes your reality."

It does so by focusing your energy and narrowing your choices. What we focus on expands, what we give our attention to grows stronger. "Our intentions cause us to pay attention to certain stimuli while totally ignoring a plethora of other possibilities," notes Mihaly Csikszentmihalyi, a professor of psychology at Claremont Graduate University. "This is the psychological process by which we construct our reality."

Susan Bishop is a good example. She was a single mom making $40,000 a year in sales when she read a book about people making six figures. "It was like a challenge," she told me. "I knew I could get there if I just brought in a certain amount of business. I started figuring out what I needed to do to bring in more sales." Within a year she had exceeded her goal.

LIVING CONSCIOUSLY

The path to higher earnings is paved with decisions, one right after the other. Do you call back a client or phone up a friend? Do you raise your rates or lower your sights? Do you make the choice that's easiest now or the one that will pay dividends down the road? Your financial destiny hinges on these daily, sometimes tiny, decisions. And it's a whole lot easier to make them when you're purposely headed in a particular direction toward a specific destination. Every time you act on your decisions, keeping your promise to yourself by honoring your intention, you build self-esteem. Stronger self-esteem only enhances your chances for success.

Marketing communication consultant Marci Blaze told me about an acquaintance who is envious of Marci's success. "I'm forever trying to tell her that I've made certain choices to achieve my success," Marci said. "For example, she's always sending me jokes on-line. If I'm at the computer, I'm working. She's forwarding jokes. I try to explain that's why she's not faring well financially. She made the choice to send jokes, I made the choice to work so I can have financial success."

WE SAY WE DO, BUT WE DON'T . . .

If intentions are so powerful, why don't they always pan out? What if you swear you want to make more money, your intent is sincere, your desire is strong, but try as you might, your paycheck remains paltry?

If this is the case, it's for this reason: *You get what you want, not what you ask for.* The distinction is critical.

Beth Sawi, chief administrative officer of Charles Schwab, described the moment she set her sights on earning six figures. "I was at Stanford with some very ambitious people, so I pushed myself into a higher bracket than I was comfortable with. Part of me said, 'I can do this.' Another part said, 'I can't.' I guess the first part was stronger."

There lies one of the biggest differences between the money-makers and the rest of the world. For lower earners, the part that says "I can't" holds the strongest sway. We all have numerous intentions, including some we aren't even aware of. You run into trouble when your expressed intentions are at odds with your unconscious ones.

When an implicit desire—say, to be comfortable—is stronger than your spoken intention—to be profitable—you'll stop yourself at every turn. You'll water down your efforts, make misguided choices, and justify your actions with a variety of excuses. You may say, and *believe*, you want to make more, but that's not the message that's reaching your brain.

If you want to know what your strongest intention is regarding money, look at your life. If cash flow is a problem, if your job pays too little, if prosperity remains elusive, if you can't seem to find the time to do what it takes, then either you have not set an intention or you actually intend *not* to be financially successful. No decision, after all, is a decision.

W H Y   W E   R E S I S T

Why in the world would any of us intend not to be successful? In part, because it's scary. Think about it. If you want something you're actually afraid of, having it isn't really what you truly want. If you're scared of heights, how likely is it you'll scale the cliff no matter how great the view is purported to be or how adamantly you swear one day you'll climb it?

There's a story about two caterpillars that spy a butterfly high overhead. One turns to the other and says, "You'll never get me up in one of those things!" In many ways we're like that caterpillar. We get a glimpse of our potential and immediately get cold feet. We may say we want something, but deep down, a muted voice is persuasively arguing, "No, you don't." Part of this is human nature, says the psychologist Abraham Maslow. "We crave and fear becoming truly ourselves." Which is what becoming a Successful High Earner is really all about.

We'll also resist success because of the way we were raised— how our families influenced us and how the culture regarded us. Their prejudices became our prototypes. Nowhere is this more apparent than in the gender myths that have delineated our roles and our relationship with money.

When Victoria Collins was hired as a college professor in 1982, she learned that her male predecessor had been paid significantly more than she was getting. She asked the dean why and was told, "Because a man has to support a family. And you're married." "I was totally satisfied with that answer," Victoria recalled. "It made perfect sense. But eventually a little voice said there's something wrong here."

Unfortunately, that little voice is routinely ignored by countless women who have been brainwashed to believe they're the ones in the wrong—as if it's unfeminine, uncouth, and unseemly to aspire to monetary gain, and downright unthinkable to discuss what we make. In fact, studies show that profit is the least important criterion for female entrepreneurs, while it's the *most* important one for men. Women are far more motivated to make a difference or be independent than to see profits grow. These are worthy goals, to be sure, but we mustn't lose sight of the larger picture. Besides, why should one preclude the other?

Joline Godfrey asked herself that very question soon after she founded Independent Means. "I started as a nonprofit and it wasn't the right model. Here I was, encouraging women to be economically empowered and I was nonprofit. I decided to walk my talk."

Joline is in the minority. Ask most women how much money they'd like to make, and you're apt to hear, "Enough to get by, enough to be comfortable." Too many women downplay the financial side of life, dismiss their low incomes as "no big deal," and adopt what some have called a "bake sale" mentality.

"Historically we women have had teeny little visions," argued Joline. "If they can raise a few hundred bucks from this bake sale, that's great. But tell them to raise ten million or a hundred million dollars and they immediately flinch. We need to practice adding zeros."

Yet, for many women who believe big money is a bad thing, hearing someone say "I want to make money" sounds tasteless, self-serving, and materialistic. Their motives seem suspect, their values seem askew. Such women automatically link the words *profit motive* with greed and self-interest, consider the concept immoral, and blame it for what's wrong with the government, politicians, and big corporations.

But did you know that in early drafts of the Declaration of Independence, Thomas Jefferson originally penned the words: "Life, Liberty, and the Pursuit of Prosperity"? Only later did he substitute "Happiness" for "Prosperity." Could we ever consider prosperity a guaranteed right, a source of happiness that's part of our heritage? Six-figure women clearly think it is.

"I believe that if you're a human being, you have the inherent right to be as wealthy as you want to be," exclaimed Lois Carrier, a financial adviser. "I had a very religious upbringing. I do believe

God intends for us to have whatever our heart desires. There's nothing wrong with that."

This mind-set was plainly missing from conversations I had with underearners. Until you're able to give yourself permission to pursue prosperity in your own right, as your right, your best intentions will remain mere pipe dreams or, at best, delusions of grandeur with no relationship to reality. Until you see profit as a virtue, not a vice, as a prerogative and not an impropriety, you won't have a sliver of hope for increasing your earnings. But a change in perception, a shift in your thinking, can transform a chronic underearner into a six-figure woman.

"When I was young, making money seemed like the wrong thing to do," corporate consultant Chris Casper told me. But when she divorced, with three kids to support, in the interest of practicality she promptly changed her mind. "I'm not ashamed to want to make a lot of money. I know my values and what I'm going to use it for. I want time to be with my kids, play the piano, do free seminars for people who can't afford them."

None of the six-figure women I talked to had any qualms about openly declaring their desire to profit. As events planner Stephanie Astic told me, "I feel great about the fact I make this money. I don't have any reservations, like it's not good to make money. I don't go to that place at all."

These women take great pleasure in wealth, joyfully reaping the psychic rewards that come with big paychecks, mindful that the more money they make, the more options they have: the more freedom they can enjoy, the more secure they feel, the more they can do for others.

One of the women I interviewed, Joan di Furia, had left a high-paying position in manufacturing to make far less as a psychologist. She was passionate about doing something that helped people. She also wanted to make money. "I have a desire in my bones to make a difference in the world," she told me. "But for me to feel successful, I need to be compensated for what I do. I love money. I can say that unabashedly. Money gives me choices, security, flexibility. When I was earning six figures, it was a blast. I got these huge checks and it was a thrill to see all those zeros."

When I interviewed corporate trainer Donalda Cormier, she, too, was mulling over a career move. "Whatever I do, I want to do it in a way that produces abundance, even more than I have now. I want to leave a financial legacy for my children, and I want financial freedom by the time I'm fifty-five. I mean, if I'm going to go for it, why wouldn't I want more?"

CRAFTING AN INTENTION—AN INSIDE JOB

That is indeed a question we should all be asking ourselves, especially when financial gain is not forthcoming. *Why wouldn't I want to make more money?* If you're not getting it, for whatever reason, chances are you don't want it. A declaration of intention, by itself, may not be enough to get you over the hump. You also need to figure out what's holding you back.

In the course of one conversation, I saw how freeing such insight could be. I was talking on the phone with a woman who was complaining that her income could be substantially higher if she didn't have kids. Then she stopped suddenly, sighed deeply, and ruefully admitted, "Listen to me! That's been my self-talk for the past two years. I can't make more because of family. How negative is that? It's my mother talking, not me. I know damn well I can work when I want and make more money. I can hire trainers, get out more products, produce the video, finish my book . . . " Her sudden awareness spawned a slew of ideas.

This is why the inner work is so critical, especially at the outset. You have to make sure your declared intention is an authentic reflection of who you are and what you want, that conflicting intentions aren't inadvertently impeding your progress, and that your intent to profit doesn't run counter to the way you were raised, the role you've assumed, or the beliefs you embrace. Over and over, these women told me how their financial success came on the heels of some personal insight.

For example, Carol Adrienne, an office worker, numerologist, tarot reader, and writer, admitted, "I spent my life in jobs where there was no money." Finally, she hit middle age, got fed up being poor, and started working on herself. "I looked at my past, my early messages around money and career. I had this thing about being invisible, not standing up for myself. I started journaling, recognizing these patterns of staying on the fence, being a victim. I kept myself out of the loop, in a second-banana role where people told me what to do. It kept me from making money. I started to see this in all areas of my life."

It was about this time she got an idea for a book that became a bestseller, *The Experiential Guide to the Celestine Prophecy.* "Ten years ago I was living in a basement with no retirement. Today I have a portfolio of stocks and own my own home," she proudly proclaimed.

Many of the women I interviewed, at various times in their careers, sat down with pen and paper—on their own, over coffee with friends, at a workshop, or with a professional—to sort through what made them tick, what kept them stuck, what they truly wanted, and the kind of work they deeply loved. One woman described the process as "an emotional and spiritual journey."

"I had to deal with who I was," she said. "I was not the poor little girl from the other side of the tracks anymore. I wanted to be in a new place, but I didn't know what that place looked like, how to act in that place, or what to do there. I had to get rid of a lot of attitudes from childhood and deal with 'Who am I?' The whole process was very revealing."

Manager Barbara Doran was in the middle of the same process when we talked. "I'm trying to figure out what will fully engage me, where my passion is," she told me. "I'm making lists. What am I good at? What are all the things in life that have made me happy? What do they have in common?"

Donalda Cormier had done the same thing years ago. "I had a very successful business but I wasn't happy. I didn't know why. I was taking a trip to New York and spent the whole time on the plane doing values work. One of the questions I asked myself was 'Why do I get up and go to work every day?' What I wrote down was: 'To have enough money to retire.' As soon as I saw that, I said, 'I'm off target here.' I realized I wasn't doing work that reflected my values. Even though I was getting paid well, I didn't feel it was providing me an opportunity to grow. That was in May. In October I left. I got back on track and then work just fell into place."

GETTING TO KNOW YOU . . .

Still, truth can be painful. Honest reflection often evokes a host of emotions—anger at all the wasted time, fear of tackling the unknown, embarrassment for the mistakes we've made, confusion about what to do next. As difficult as it may be, we *must* lift the veils—look at ourselves directly and tell the truth about what we see—for change to occur. This became an ongoing theme throughout my interviews: women telling me that once they got a glimpse of their truth, once they realized their deepest desires and highest aspirations, they experienced a literal turn of events. I was fascinated to hear how many of them took the time to figure out not just how to boost their earnings, but how to do it in a way that fit who they were. While monetary gain was clearly their goal, it would be a hollow victory if they weren't living full lives. The secret to becoming a Successful High Earner, and not a hard-driven one, is to keep these dual intentions always in mind.

"I'm a huge believer in intention," said real estate executive Gail Sturm. "And not just to make money but to have balance." Finding balance is a tricky feat in the six-figure world, but it was clearly possible. As one woman told me: "We have time to do everything that's important to us. The secret is to be decisive about what's really important."

I found it very heartening to hear how many of the women I interviewed spent extended periods trying to figure out the lifestyle they hoped to create. Many had done various kinds of value-clarification exercises and every one told me how those experiences were literally life-changing.

One very memorable story came from management consultant Carol Anderson, who, during a personal growth workshop, was asked a most provocative question: If you were on your deathbed, looking back at your life, what would make you feel happiest and most satisfied with how you lived? From her response emerged a list of her most pressing priorities.

"Before I had these priorities, I was easily distracted by things that momentarily interested me. For example, shortly after doing this workshop, a man starting a business in China asked me to be on the board. They were going to have an all-expense-paid weekend in San Francisco. Now, there was a time I would have dashed off and done it, because it sounded interesting and I was proud to be asked. But Chinese business is not one of my priorities. It could've been fun. I would've met interesting people. But it would have taken me away from my partner, the book I'm writing, things that are really important. So it was easy to say no."

Beth Sawi reported a similar experience. This Charles Schwab executive, who wrote *Coming Up for Air*, a book about balance, followed the advice she gave to her readers: Figure out the five things that matter most and don't worry about the rest (her top five: "good health, work that counts, close family, robust spirituality, and close friends"). When her life started getting out of whack, she knew exactly what was wrong. She and her husband had bought a second home, a vineyard in Napa.

"So now I had six things on my list," Beth told me. "I realized I was pushing friends to number six, feeling very conflicted. I know I have to make some changes."

Another woman, who took a goal-setting class, told me that she carries a list of her priorities in her Franklin Planner. "If they're not at the top of my mind, I tend to be more reactive with life."

To help you discern and shape your intentions around money, try the following techniques:

- *Write it down.* When I was a career counselor, I always gave these three exercises to clients. The opportunity for directed self-reflection provides a wealth of information about what you need to feel fulfilled in a job and in life.
  Value-Clarification Exercise (page 103)
  The Feedback Sheet (page 105)
  Finding Your Motivational Pattern (page 105)
- *Watch yourself around money.* "Money is like a Rorschach test," I once heard a psychologist say. "We give it its meaning." For one week, look for the meaning you attribute to money. Observe your attitudes, beliefs, thoughts, feelings, decisions, and choices around anything financial. Do this without judgment or criticism. Journal about your insights.
- *Do daily affirmations.* Affirmations are positive statements expressed as if they've already happened. For example: "I *am* a

six-figure woman." "I welcome abundance in my life." (Any of the final fifteen statements in the underearning quiz on pages 68–70 can be used as powerful affirmations.) Write them down. Post them in full view. Say them out loud as often as possible. Every day I look at the yellow Post-It note by the screen of my computer and remind myself: "I *am* making $125,000."

As affirmation enthusiast Beth Chapman told me, "The more often I hear the words coming out of my mouth, the more I internalize them, and the more my psyche knows they're going to happen." (You'll read more about affirmations in chapter 5.)

A declaration of intention is only the first strategy of financial success, but it is the most crucial one of all. When you're clear about who you are and what you want, it's amazing the things that can happen. When your declared intentions are aligned with your deepest values and highest priorities, when conflicting objectives cease to control you, you'll have harnessed within you a powerful force that literally pulls you toward your desired future. Before turning the page, take a moment to declare your intention, using your own words, but saying in effect that it's time to earn more money. This intention, said with conviction, places you squarely in the driver's seat, all set to travel through each of the following six strategies.

VALUE-CLARIFICATION EXERCISE

Values are those desired qualities that give your life meaning. They are essential to satisfaction and happiness. Below is a list of values. Circle the ten that are most important to you—based on your first gut-level reaction.

Then cross out five, leaving the five values that you simply couldn't live without. Rank the remaining five 1 to 5 in order of importance.

Achievement	Knowledge
Adventure	Leadership
Beauty	Learning
Being free	Leaving a legacy
Being generous	Leisure
Brotherhood	Life partner
Charity	Love
Comfort	Making a difference
Community	Parenting
Creativity	Patriotism
Dignity	Peace
Discovery	Physical activity
Family	Power
God	Retirement
Growth	Security
Happiness	Seeing the world
Health	Self-discipline
Honesty	Self-esteem
Honor	Service
Humility	Simplicity
Independence	Spirituality
Individuality	Strength
Influence	Success
Integrity	Time alone
Intimacy	Truth
Justice	Using my talents
Kindness	

THE FEEDBACK SHEET

Feedback from others who interact with us in different circumstances can be extremely enlightening. Make four copies of this sheet. Give one copy each to four people whose feedback you would welcome: friends, colleagues, family. Ask them to fill out the form as honestly and objectively as they can. And don't look over their shoulder while they do it!

1. What do you see as my major personality strengths?
2. What do you see as my marketable skills?
3. What kind of environment do you see me working in?
4. What do you think I need in a job?
5. What do you see in me that I probably don't see in myself?

FINDING YOUR MOTIVATIONAL PATTERN

Step I. Divide your life into thirds. (If you are 42, you'll come up with three age groups: 1–14, 15–28, 29–42.) Then let your thoughts begin to drift. Recall some of your past accomplishments: the things you did well, enjoyed doing, and felt good about regardless of what anyone else thought. These experiences must be something you did, not something you watched others doing. It can be anything from learning to tie your shoes to reupholstering a chair, from finding a job to writing a poem, from planning a party for four or a banquet for four hundred. The important thing here is that you felt good about the activity, enjoyed doing it, and did it well.

Step II. Create a chart. Try to come up with at least three achievements for each of your three age groups.

Your Age	*The Experience*	*The Reason*
Your age at the time of the experience.	Describe in detail exactly what you did to accomplish the experience.	What made it a success for you? (Two people can have the same experience but find it rewarding for different reasons. For example, when you wrote stories as a kid, you loved the compliments, but I really enjoyed the act of creating things by myself.)

Step III. Examine the experiences listed and look for a pattern. What skills, interests, rewards, and kinds of relationships are repeated in all the stories? This is called your motivational pattern. *It is what "turns you on," gets you going, and keeps you stimulated. If you put these ingredients together, you can see what is missing in your life or what you need to have in your next job. For example, if helping people motivates you and your day is spent behind a computer, you can see why you're miserable.*

5

STRATEGY #2:
LETTING GO OF THE LEDGE

*If I get stuck in who I am now, I will never blossom into who
I might yet become. I need to practice the gentle art of letting go.*
—SAM KEEN, AUTHOR

God, give me guts.
—ANONYMOUS

There's a story about a mountain climber who misses her footing and slides down the rock toward the edge of the cliff. Just before she's about to go over, she grabs hold of the ledge and hangs there, suspended in midair. Desperately, she cries out, "Lord, help me. Please come to my rescue!"

The Lord answers, "Yes, Sadie, I can help you, but first there's one thing you must do."

"Oh Lord," Sadie says, "I'll do anything. What must I do?"

And the Lord answers, "Sadie, you have to let go of that ledge."

That's exactly what every woman I spoke to was called to do as she made her way to higher earnings. She had to *let go of the ledge.* Their ledges took many forms, both concrete and intangible—from unfulfilling jobs to unpleasant relationships, from inappropriate goals to inaccurate beliefs, from damaging habits to detrimental emotions.

This is an essential, though often overlooked, strategy for financial success, rooted in a principle so simple it's basic common sense: *You must let go of where you are to get to where you want to go.* Clinging to the security of the familiar prevents us from discovering what awaits us in the future. The ledges in our lives offer the illusion of safety, but in truth their only value is to keep us hanging, their only reward is burnout, boredom, financial lack, or personal frustration.

Still, as the parable suggests, carrying out this strategy entails incredible trust. Letting go of the ledge is like dropping into the abyss, having the faith you'll land on your feet with no real assurance that will actually happen. Every woman I spoke to, at various times in her career, had to let go of established routines, steady incomes, steadfast beliefs, or long-standing relationships. They let go with their fingers crossed, their hopes high, long on optimism but short on guarantees. This wasn't something that came naturally. Like the woman in the story, they'll all agree. Letting go of the ledge takes a whole lot of nerve.

"It was like jumping off a cliff," said Karen Page about her decision to quit corporate life to become a full-time author. "To leave the comfort of a company, a steady paycheck, to jump into the unknown, it felt so scary."

"What made you leave?" I asked. Her answer was one I often heard from Successful High Earners: not just to *make* more but to *become* more.

"It was really about self-expression, achieving my potential, not about what my paycheck was. At first I didn't make six figures. I think that's important for anyone taking the risk. You're going to make some sacrifices, but it's possible to come out the other side and do it. I did."

Every successful woman I interviewed, when she finally let go (hard as it was), cited that single act as the springboard to higher earnings and happier times.

"When I finally told my husband I was leaving him, it was like the cage door opened and I flew out. I made one phone call and forty-eight hours later I was hired at six figures. It was a miracle," recalled Nicole Young, a former housewife who is now a senior vice president of Charles Schwab. However, she readily admitted, "It was the hardest thing I ever did. I had to give up the security of depending on my doctor husband to provide for me and start trusting myself. I was stuck for a long time."

One thing is for sure. The concept of letting go is far easier to talk about than to execute. Many six-figure women admitted remaining in unfavorable situations, some holding tighter or dangling longer than others. And when they eventually did let go, it wasn't without second thoughts or stabs of doubt.

It took management consultant Carol Anderson two years to dissolve a business relationship even though it was not healthy. "Those were the worst years I ever had financially. I didn't have a single client in sight, only four thousand dollars in the bank, and no idea what I'd do next," she said.

Finally, when she screwed up the courage to leave the situation, she got a call "out of the blue" from a colleague, which resulted in a slew of business. She marks her financial success from the moment she stopped doing something that wasn't good for her and trusted her resourcefulness to figure out what to do next. "I believe that life works when you're true to yourself and it doesn't when you're not. But I have to keep reminding myself of that all the time."

We all do. These interviews provided continual reminders for me that, as another woman put it, "when I do what's right for me, the universe supplies something. It never fails."

"NATURE ABHORS A VACUUM"

These women's comments might sound a tad mystical, but it's hard to argue with the facts. Amazing coincidences so often occur as soon as people let go. And there's a perfectly valid explanation. This is the inevitable outcome of the first two strategies working in tandem. While "intention" is a magnet that attracts what we want, "letting go" provides the space for our desire to manifest.

I heard from one woman after another that once they let go, once they stopped holding on to what they *thought* they *had* to have and instead practiced nonattachment, stuff miraculously happened. Many described the act of letting go as a turning point, after which everything else just fell into place.

Letting go was certainly the turning point for a woman I interviewed who was on the verge of accepting a CEO position. One night, she told me, "I woke up in a cold sweat thinking I didn't really want this job. I didn't want to run something, I wanted to solve problems—which is what consultants do, not CEOs."

Three days after she turned down the offer, a friend called and asked her for help. "Three days later! She was my first client. The universe just lines up when you're headed in the right direction. I'm making more money than I ever did as a corporate executive."

The same thing happened to musician Bette Sussman. She gave up the enviable and lucrative job of touring the world with Whitney Houston because life on the road was way too exhausting. Almost immediately, she landed an even more lucrative gig writing music for a TV show in her hometown of New York.

"I really believe by cutting back I opened a new door which earned me more money," Bette explained. "That was a revelation for me—that you have to close certain doors to open new ones."

Many women confirmed the truth of this cliché: When one door closes, another opens. But you may not see the open door right away. You may even have to go searching for that new door, trusting it's there, despite what people tell you. And you won't always find it as fast as you'd like.

Makeup artist Kris Evans recalled a pivotal point in her career: "I was supposed to work on this film, but it didn't pay enough. Part of me was like, 'Oh my God, I should. Money. Money. Money.' The other part said, 'It just doesn't feel right, and I have to trust something else will come.' I sent my résumé to a major film that was shooting in Utah. I saw it advertised in a trade magazine.

"Everyone says you never get big jobs by sending résumés. You have to know someone. I thought, What do I have to lose? They called me. They wanted me to interview to head the show, be the key makeup. This was a huge opportunity, much bigger than the movie I turned down. And they hired me. That was the start of my career in big films. It was *Con Air*, a hundred-million-dollar movie. And I headed it. It put me in another echelon."

TURNING DOWN LESS

Regardless of the circumstances, we'll remain underearners until we firmly resolve that settling for less is no longer an option. Anita Saville left a high-paying corporate job to find she earned a whole lot less as a freelance writer, until she figured out why—she kept agreeing to do work that paid very little.

"You gradually realize that if you take something that doesn't pay much, and then something comes along that pays a lot more, you won't be able to do it because you're tied into a lower fee. The lower rate doesn't necessarily mean less work. In fact, mostly it's a lot *more* work." She now makes significantly more than she likely ever could have made in the corporate world.

Anita's words struck a familiar chord. I regularly accepted speaking engagements for nominal fees. I guess I was just grateful to be asked. But after a few of these interviews, I made a vow to myself: I would only work at my going rate, which was very reasonable by industry standards. I have to tell you, it was a humbling experience. No one wanted to pay what I was asking. Not a single person. Those rejections sent me into a tailspin of self-doubt. Here I was writing a book on making money, and I couldn't get anyone to pay me a decent sum. I began questioning my decision, doubting my skills, and wondering if I'd ever work again. This period, during which I was truly tested, lasted about six months. All the while, I was interviewing six-figure women. They were my saving grace. So many women told me they'd had similar experiences, that rejection was part of the process. "It's the fear factor," one woman explained. "Every time you turn work down, you get scared it'll all dry up. But it never does. Not if you stick with it, and you're fairly valued."

I stood firm, and slowly invitations to speak at my advertised rates began coming in. Sticking to my guns, and my fees, sent my income soaring higher than anything else I could ever have done. I'm forever grateful for the lesson these women taught me: *Those who are satisfied with crumbs will never have the whole loaf.*

When Vivian Carpenter, suddenly widowed at age twenty-six, began looking for a job, she went to a headhunter. "I told him I wanted a job that paid thirty thousand dollars. He came back with offers for twenty-five thousand dollars. I told him no. I wouldn't work for less than thirty thousand dollars because it wouldn't put me on the right track or give me authority or exposure. He told me I was vain. I didn't even know what the word meant. I grew up in the inner city of Detroit and had a very limited vocabulary. I had to look it up."

IT NEVER ENDS!

Vivian did get a job that paid what she wanted. Years afterward, with a Ph.D. under her belt, she was offered a plum professorship at Florida A&M University, but refused it because, again, the offer felt too low. "It wasn't the money. It was the tracking. If I'd taken less, I wouldn't be on track to be the dean's successor, which is what I really wanted." Five years later, however, "out of the blue," the dean called and made Vivian "an offer I couldn't refuse. It was the right amount [close to six figures] and the right position, as a director, running the department."

But the job quickly became too consuming. Vivian was commuting between Michigan and Florida, working seventy-hour weeks, sorely neglecting her family, feeling frazzled and trapped.

Vivian's career trajectory brings up an important point: *Letting go is never-ending.* It's something that the women I spoke to are called to do repeatedly, every time they reach a pinnacle and want to climb higher, or when they hit a snag and need to change course. Sometimes they have to let go of the very thing they've worked so hard to achieve in the first place. That was Vivian's dilemma. How did she resolve it?

"I got on my knees and prayed," Vivian said. "I asked God to bring more balance in my life and move me in the direction I needed to go. That's when I realized I wasn't trapped in the job as director. I could go back to a regular faculty position."

The moment Vivian released the directorship, she received something even better. The dean created a brand-new position for her and allowed her to take a year off. Today, Vivian is president of her own firm, sits on several corporate boards, spends more time with her family, and makes "in the high six figures."

"It wasn't until I was willing to give up everything that I was able to create the conditions that have let me be truly successful. A lot of people feel trapped. They aren't. They only need to let go to move forward." And to achieve balance.

GIVING UP GOOD

Still, the temptation to stay put, no matter how bad things get, is huge. Who wants to rock the boat, shake up the status quo, willingly plunge into the chaos of change. It's especially tough to let go if what we're giving up isn't all that bad to begin with. When I sold my successful career counseling firm in Kansas City years ago and moved west to become a writer, I kept a quote of Carl Jung's framed on my desk for reassurance: "For better to come, good must stand aside."

Those words have been prophetic for so many women I interviewed, who gave up something good to grab hold of something better. I had such admiration for these women. As far as I'm concerned, leaving the acceptable to step into the void is the ultimate act of courage.

"It would've been more comfortable to remain a scientist," said Kraft marketing director Doreen Stephans, formerly a chemical engineer. "In science, there's always a right answer. You have a formula and you apply it. In marketing there is no right answer. I had to change my thinking, become comfortable with unknowns, making decisions based on eighty percent, even fifty percent of the information. But my salary doubled immediately. I never would've gotten there so quickly as an engineer."

Nor would investment banker Miriam have been as financially successful if she had continued running an art gallery. "I loved the art world. When I left, I was very afraid that I was going to lose all the people in that world that I'd grown close to. And I have to some extent. But where it's mattered, I've retained the most important relationships. It was the biggest risk I took, losing relationships. But I knew it was time for a change."

It also became obvious to Harriett Simon Salinger, after going belly up in her seminar business, that she, too, needed to let go to get back on her feet. "I left New York and my entire support system and drove across the country," she told me. "I intuitively knew I had to make a radical change. If I hadn't, I would've kept on being a therapist, stayed in the self-development business, doing groups. In California, I wasn't licensed, so I couldn't fall into that trap."

Similarly, Tracey Scott saw an enormous jump in salary the year she moved from Atlanta to California in her job with a major telecommunications firm. "This was a huge move. I was moving away from family. I knew only one person in California. It was an expensive place. There were so many unknowns, so many hard ties to break. But I knew I was ready for a change. When the opportunity came, I took it."

MENTAL MOLDS

Sometimes, however, what we need to relinquish isn't readily apparent. It's not something we can physically touch or actually see. Just as I began writing this chapter, I got an excited call from my friend Kitty Reeve.

"I made six figures this year," she announced with a mixture of pride and astonishment.

My jaw dropped at the news. I knew Kitty as an average earner, a freelance writer and photographer. But last year, at age fifty-eight, she turned a sideline interest into a thriving business, becoming an Internet consultant in on-line community, content, and strategy.

"How did you do it?" I asked, absolutely shocked.

Her answer was immediate. "I realized I had to put aside the myth that money was bad. I used to think there's a limited supply and if you have more then someone else has less. If I do OK, some woman is homeless. I wouldn't ever let myself make money until I changed my attitude. I was blocking myself."

Indeed, I have never met an underearner who wasn't blocking herself with erroneous thinking or misguided notions. Letting go of our "mental molds" (as one woman called them) is the crucial challenge for each of us on the path to higher earnings. Even if the ledge we cling to is an external situation, there's always an internal authority governing our decisions, something in our psyches, a belief or attitude, that's putting us down, holding us back, keeping us hanging. In every spiritual discipline, the master's first task is to tear down the novice's view of the world. In Zen, the metaphor most often used is the overflowing teacup. We must first empty the container before we can refill it. Similarly, if our minds are full of limiting thoughts, there's no room for the expansive ones. Success can only come when there's space for it to enter.

I had some very moving conversations with women who recognized they had to reject their frame of reference if they were to ever get ahead. An author had to let go of her addiction to fame; an executive, her craving for approval; a banker, her angst about being incompetent; and a business owner, her rage at her ex-husband. A highly stressed entrepreneur had to give up a childhood belief that she wasn't lovable unless she was productive. Just about every one who grew up poor had to quit thinking that she wasn't deserving, that money was bad, or that she'd become superficial and materialistic if she had any. More than a few had to stop depending on another in order to find herself.

"I had to grow up," said Barbara Blair, now CEO of a multimillion-dollar business. When she filed for divorce at age twenty-nine, her father-in-law offered her a large sum of money to stay in her marriage. She refused, even though it meant supporting her kids on food stamps while she looked for a job. "It was very hard, but I couldn't stay a protected child forever."

Barbara realized what we all must grasp if we're going to get to six figures: To *really* change your financial situation, you have to let go of that part of yourself that stands in the way of greater abundance. All these women had to break their mental molds, empty their overflowing cups, let loose of their ledges. Only then were they free to make different choices from a fresh perspective.

THE STUCK FACTOR

How do you know when you've been holding on too long to a ledge? There's one irrefutable clue. Whenever you feel stuck, it's time to let go. And invariably, what you need to let go of is the very thing you are most afraid to release. It's the fear, not the circumstances, that keeps us trapped.

"I don't think people get stuck," declared publishing consultant Jodee Blanco, when we talked about not being able to take the leap. "I think that's another way of saying they're scared. I'm speaking from experience. I was working for a Madison Avenue firm. The money was terrible. I needed a break. But I was terrified to quit. Meanwhile, I was twenty-seven. I helped put eight books onto the bestseller list. I was one of the most visible celebrity publishing PR people in New York. Yet I was still deeply frightened that if I left the firm, I'd never get another job, and my employer, whom I cared for deeply, would feel betrayed."

When she finally left, Jodee discovered a piece of timeless wisdom. "I'll tell you this. The fear is worse than what you go through when you do it." In four days, she had $30,000 worth of business. Within a year she was representing major motion pictures, Fortune 500 companies, and top publishing houses.

"But I'm facing it again," she confided. "I'm working too hard. I want to tell my partner I'm leaving to simplify my life. Once again, I'm terrified of the same things. How am I going to pay my mortgage? How will my partner respond? Will she freak out, sue me, jump off the roof? Even though my head knows she probably won't, I'm scared nonetheless.

"I think women are so choked with fear and anxiety we can't move. But I also know you can't make money without courage. It just won't happen. I'll always have that fear of hurting people. The only thing I can do is be aware of it and march forward sensitively and with determination."

(When I talked to Jodee again, months later, she had taken a leave of absence from the partnership to create her own consulting business and was delighted to report that the money is better, the freedom is delicious, and the relationship with her partner has survived beautifully.)

Fear and anxiety are to financial success what labor pains are to childbirth—an unpleasant, but unavoidable, part of the process. Every time we let go, there's always a loss—an actual loss like a job or a spouse, or an emotional loss like stability or security. And loss produces anxiety because it poses a threat (real or imagined, it makes no difference) to our essence or core, our very survival. It's your ability to tolerate and push through anxiety that gets you to your goal. But it's not easy. It's never easy.

"Leaving my position at the bank was harder than getting a divorce," said a woman who recently joined a start-up. "All of a sudden I didn't have an identity."

Letting go often leaves us feeling vulnerable, volatile, and fragile. Rather than hazard the instability of change, we lean on the ledges as if they were crutches, finding all kinds of reasons why we need to stay right where we are. The economist John Kenneth Galbraith put it this way: "Given the choice between changing and proving there's no need to do so, almost everybody will get busy on the proof." Perhaps that's why many of us need to have our fingers pried loose before we'll finally let go.

That was the case with Beth Chapman, a PR consultant who spent years in a corporate job that made her miserable. "I can't tell you how disheartened and maligned I felt about the way I was treated, what a drag it was on my self-esteem."

"Would you have left if you hadn't been fired?" I asked.

"No, I wouldn't have left. I had two boys—one leaving for college, one four years behind him—and a huge mortgage. I would never have guessed I could earn enough money to keep the house. But when they let me go, a piece of me said, 'You'll never have a chance to try again to start a business. Give it a shot.'" Her shot at self-employment made her a six-figure woman at age forty-eight.

Many of us will have to be pushed before we are ready to fly, no matter how bad things get. As one woman said of her reluctance to change, "Everyplace I've ever been has my claw marks all over it."

"We fear that if we relinquish our stuff, even if it is getting in our way, there will be nothing left of us. This is the primary reason that letting go is so difficult," says Susanna McMahon in the *Portable Therapist*. "The other reason is we're still trying to please our parents."

I couldn't help but laugh when Mary Helen Gillespie told me why she was so reluctant to leave journalism to create a consulting firm that would triple her income. "I was forty-two, married, and scared to tell my parents I was quitting my job to start my own business. I felt like a junior in high school telling them I got a D in chemistry."

As ridiculous as that may sound, it's no less absurd than the reasons some of us have conjured up to justify the status quo. How often, when we should be releasing, do we find ourselves resisting? You know you're in resistance if, when you set an intention to profit, you start procrastinating, forgetting, blaming, becoming too busy, making excuses, losing interest, creating distractions, or scaring yourself with worst-case scenarios. Resistance is normal. Notice it, but *still* be willing to loosen your grip.

When I asked my interviewees about their biggest regrets, "staying too long" was the one most often cited. How many women told me, their voices heavy with remorse, that they should have followed their intuition and left their marriages, their jobs, or various situations much sooner than they did.

Does this mean we should all go out and pursue whatever wild idea pops into our minds, whether or not it is rooted in reality? The answer is a qualified yes . . . if something inside us is spurring us in that direction. Even if it doesn't work out as expected, it may be just the thing we need to do to get us where we need to go. The key here is to listen to our intuitive urgings instead of our preconceived notions about what's practical or reasonable. Being overly realistic or inordinately logical can be as much of a liability as low self-esteem. They all serve the same god, fear, and will swiftly suppress any impulse to risk.

Most of us know when it's time to let go; we're just not ready to admit it. Many women told me, as Donalda Cormier did after finally leaving an unhealthy business partnership, "My intuition told me from the beginning something was askew. I let my logic override my gut. It was a good learning for me. I learned to pay attention to my intuition. When I meet someone now, if my gut is saying 'Danger! Danger!' I don't override it. I trust it, even if there is no logical basis."

Still, paying attention to your intuition is one thing, acting on it yet another. When it comes right down to it, we'll cling fiercely to lack and limitation rather than endure the anxiety intrinsic to change.

HOW DO YOU LET GO?

Here's what I've learned from these six-figure women. There are certain steps you can take to facilitate the process of letting go, which will make it a little easier, less traumatic, and more rewarding.

- *Keep your intention in front of you.*
  Inspired by a book on high earners, Susan Bishop knew the only chance she had of making six figures was to stop drawing a salary and go completely on commission. The thought terrified her. She was a single mom with a five-year-old daughter. What if she couldn't make it? "I had some tearful moments when business wasn't forthcoming. Even my boss said, 'Why are you doing this? Your first concern should be your daughter.' I said, 'It is. I'm doing this so we can have a better life.' He said, 'What if you can't make it?' I said, 'I have to.' I had a lot of determination."

Intense determination is the inevitable by-product of a solid intention. It's what gave these women the courage to let go sooner rather than later. Take Kitty Reeve, my friend who stopped thinking money was bad and started making big bucks. What actually prompted her change of heart was the sudden realization that she was approaching sixty and had saved nothing for retirement. For the first time in her life, she had a profit motive.

"I'd never thought about retirement before. I love my work, so I always thought I'd work forever. I was so naive. I didn't realize your energy level changes, and even if you love your work, you don't want to work forever," she told me. "I saw I had better make some money."

Kitty's intention to "make some money" is what forced her to rethink her attitude about money.

- *Figure out what you need to let go of.*

Most of us live by default, never reflecting on what we really do or don't want. But I saw that high-earning women put a lot of thought into letting go.

Karen Page was making six figures in a corporate job that wasn't fulfilling. "I thought the money would make me happy. It didn't," she said, repeating what so many others also told me. She looked at the long hours, constant travel, working weekends, projects she had no enthusiasm for, and decided, "This wasn't what I wanted to do on a daily basis for five more years. I had to figure out what I really valued. What would give me greater satisfaction? I came to see how much I valued independence, being my own boss, being self-determined, being creative."

Financial adviser and author Eileen Michaels told me about a process she used when she couldn't decide whether or not to accept a tempting offer from a competing firm.

"I was so worried about everyone else's feelings that I was ignoring my own," she said. "So I said to myself, 'If I wasn't concerned with everyone else's opinion, what would I want to do?' Once everyone else's voice stopped, I could hear my own voice and I knew I couldn't possibly stay. I made the decision that day."

Entrepreneur Susan Davis, who had already failed at launching a national women's magazine, was scared to take on another start-up. "I had to put the full focus of my attention on releasing the restraints. I realized my self-defeating beliefs were getting in the way—beliefs that I have too little money, too few contacts, too low self-confidence. I've never done this business before so what makes me think I can be successful? I had to brainstorm with myself to overcome those internal objections."

At one of my workshops on underearning, Tanya told me: "Before this group, I would have never considered not being a teacher. I have a lot invested in this work—my identity, my pension, my security. But now, after doing the exercises, I see I have all these screwed-up beliefs. It's like I have to take them out of the box and say to each one, 'I don't need you anymore.' "

The challenge is to identify what you don't need anymore. You can do it by asking yourself some questions and being brutally honest and highly sensitive to your first intuitive responses:

What do I need to have in my life to feel deeply satisfied?

What do I know in my heart is keeping me from feeling satisfied and successful?

What situations, relationships, beliefs, attitudes, thoughts, feelings, and choices have I made that are no longer serving me?

If I had a year to live, where would I be? Who would I be with? What would I be doing?

• *Replace the negative with something affirmative.*

In his classic book *Money Is My Friend,* Phil Laut describes what he calls the Earning Law. "All wealth is created by the human mind. Increasing your wealth is a matter of increasing the quality of your thoughts." He suggests asking yourself, "What have I been thinking that has created my life the way it is? List the ten most negative ideas you have about money. Then invert them into affirmations."

This is what Lois Carrier, a financial planner, did. "I recognized I was giving myself negative messages and those determined what I was getting. So when I started putting positive messages in my head, positive things started happening. I did affirmations like 'I'm comfortable with money,' 'I am worthy,' 'I don't feel guilty when I have money.' I've been doing these affirmations for the last seven years very effectively. I write them out. I read them every morning and night. I've kept them all. I'll be saying one and I'll recognize, Wait, that's already happened! It's amazing to me how far I've come when I look at my old affirmations."

Consultant Carin Gendell did something similar though less

structured, when she gave up a very-high-powered position to go out on her own. "My title had always branded me as someone important. Suddenly it was gone. That was very hard on my self-esteem," she admitted. But instead of dwelling on what she'd lost, Carin concentrated on what lay ahead. "I started focusing on what I was learning, how happy I was, the time with my family, the flexibility I have, and all the people I'm helping. Helping clients became more important than being a significant person in some hierarchy. It was more gratifying to add value than to impress someone with my title."

- *Take your time.*

Who says you have to rush into anything? Sometimes it's better to gradually let go of a ledge than to take a flying leap. That's often what most of the women I talked to did. Instead of going cold turkey, they released their grip little bits at a time.

"What helped for me was to ease into it," said Karen Page about her decision to become a full-time author. "I worked on my first book as a part-time project with my husband while also working a full-time job. It was an evolutionary process. I kind of tiptoed into writing in the evening and on weekends, until we had a book contract and enough guts to leave our day jobs and become full-time authors."

The truth is, letting go seldom happens overnight. Even if it looks to an outsider like an impulsive act or a sudden insight, the ideas about leaving have probably been simmering on the back burner for quite some time. And this is just as well, for abrupt change can be disorienting and overwhelming.

- *Feel the fear.*

  Feel the fear and still persevere—you'll notice this six-figure secret weaves its way through every strategy and everyone's story. I remember a woman on the verge of a big change telling me she was a bundle of nerves, an absolute wreck, even though she knew it was a great opportunity.

  "What are you going to do?" I asked her. Her reply: "I'm going to be in fear until I'm not in fear anymore."

  Trying to escape this tension through alcohol, overwork, apathy, or denial can turn fear and anxiety into destructive forces. Acknowledging the fear and acting in the face of it, on the other hand, makes enormous creativity possible.

  The late psychologist Rollo May, author of *The Meaning of Anxiety,* tells us the discomfort of anxiety has a definite purpose: "Anxiety illuminates experiences that we could otherwise run away from. It stimulates us to find new ways of meeting problems."

  I vividly recall when I first spoke to the woman, a direct marketing specialist, who was so burnt out, she told me between sobs, "Every part of me is saying, 'Just stop. Walk away. Close down the business.' But I can't. It feels so irresponsible." Yet when I called her back three months later that's precisely what she had done.

  "I surrendered to the whole experience," she said, her voice full of energy and enthusiasm. "Instead of resisting it, I just said, 'OK, I'm going to get as depressed as I possibly can.'" In the course of her reflection, she realized what was missing: She wasn't having any fun. "So I stopped doing all the stuff that wasn't any fun, the boring projects, the 'diva' clients. I sat around for several weeks with nothing to do and made that OK." When she literally let go of everything, the ideas began flowing, and with renewed energy, she took her business in a whole new direction.

• *At least be willing to let go.*

Sometimes all you need is the willingness to let go. "I really believe you can manifest what you want, like getting a six-figure job in forty-eight hours," declared Nicole Young, who was hired that quickly after her divorce. "You have to believe you can do it—visualize it, affirm it—then let it go. You have to be unattached, release it to the universe. You have to believe in it and literally let it go."

When Stephanie Astic started her events company, she had such a rough time that her mother suggested, "Maybe you ought to let it go." But she'd worked so hard and hadn't come close to reaching her goals, so she went to her priest in despair. He told her to pray every day for as much work as she could handle. If her prayers weren't answered, then she'd know to let go. She followed his advice.

"I prayed every day, 'Please God, let me know if this is what I'm supposed to be doing. I know I can handle a full plate. Please fill it, or if it is not meant to be, then I'll figure that out.'"

Within two weeks, she was inundated with work. "It came from the sky. I'd get calls from people who didn't even remember how they heard about me, clients who wanted me to produce events. It was so amazing."

JUST THE BEGINNING

This strategy will produce amazing results, but letting go is only the beginning. "All change begins with an ending," says Bill Bridges, the author of *Transitions*. And T. S. Eliot echoes, "The end is where we start from." Now that you've stepped up to the plate, you're set to go. But when the opportunities arise, as they inevitably will, you'll have to be willing to run with them. That's where the next strategy comes into play.

6

STRATEGY #3:
GET IN THE GAME

Your work is to discover your work, and then,
with all your heart, to give yourself to it.
—BUDDHA

The mighty oak was once a little nut that held its ground.
—ANONYMOUS

The day started just like every other. Barbara Blair was on her way to another job interview as a medical technician when suddenly she saw something that would change her life forever—a woman getting out of a taxi.

"This woman was wearing a blue suit, white shirt, little tie, blue pumps, carrying a briefcase. She was impeccable," recalled Barbara, then newly divorced with no money and two kids. "I looked at her and said, 'That's what I'm going to be.' That became my model of a businesswoman. I went out and got a blue suit, the whole getup. That's how I started."

Sure enough, in four months, Barbara had a job in copier sales making $40,000. By year's end, she was making $60,000. These days she's drawing seven figures as CEO of CyberStaff America, Ltd., a company she founded in 1995.

Spotting that woman was a defining moment in Barbara's career, the moment she made her declaration of intention. But obviously it took more than a blue suit and a solid intention to go from dirt-poor to self-made millionaire. When I asked how she became successful so quickly, she summed up a critical strategy in a few choice words: "I got in the game and stayed in the game. There's no other way.

"Sometimes it's not easy. Sometimes you don't win. Sometimes you feel like a loser. But if you stay with it, be consistent, you'll hit an upward cycle."

This straightforward strategy—*get in the game and stay in the game*—may sound simple, even self-explanatory, but don't let it fool you. The game Barbara refers to has very specific rules. Unless you play by these rules, you don't stand a chance. Though these rules haven't been formally laid out for us, I noticed that high-earning women have them all figured out. Here are the seven rules that I gleaned from my conversations with them.

RULE ONE: DECIDE WHICH GAME TO PLAY

"There are two games in life," motivational speaker Larry Wilson once told me in an interview. "The one most of us are playing, called Not to Lose, is an avoidance game. We're so afraid of taking risks, looking bad, that we never really win."

People who play Not to Lose have one intention—to play it safe. No matter how much they say they want success, if they're playing Not to Lose, what they're really after is comfort, convenience, and relief. If you want to know how this game is played, just talk to any underearner. I remember a woman in one of my groups moaning, "Getting out there, saying I'm an artist, promoting my work, just paralyzes me. It's fear of rejection, I'm sure. I don't know how else to explain it."

The desire to avoid fear (whether it's fear of rejection or of disapproval, of success or of failure) is what keeps most of us in the Not to Lose game—and in low-paying jobs. Successful High Earners, on the other hand, play the game Larry Wilson calls To Win.

"You know why I'm good at my job?" Karen Sheridan once told her boss after she lost a big client. "Because I love winning way more than I hate losing. I never focus on the losses, only the wins."

To six-figure women, losses are as inevitable as ants at a picnic. And they don't let those losses ruin their plans. They focus on winning and not on defeat. Oddly enough, the object of the game is not winning per se. The whole point is to do your best and go the distance. "To win," Larry Wilson explained, *"you go as far as you can using all that you've got."*

Barbara Blair described how the game is played. "If you want something, you have to go for it. No obstacle can stand in your way. You may not get where I've gotten," she said, referring to her $20 million business, "But you can get close to your goal. And after you get close, you take a deep breath and go further. When you don't go for it, you don't get it."

No one I interviewed will tell you it's easy. And many will offer a warning. There's a strong tendency when fear and stress come up, as they invariably do, to slip back to what feels safe, into the game Not to Lose. It's a natural response, even for some Successful High Earners. The whole key to this strategy is to recognize, as quickly as possible, that you're playing to be safe and *not* to succeed. These setbacks are to be expected. Just about every woman experienced them, especially early in her career. But eventually each one recognized that if she wanted to up her earnings she had to change her game from Not to Lose to play To Win.

For example, Michele Page, a young divorcée, was determined to be an artist. "I went to the art institute just to see what would happen," Michele recalled. "The woman [in admissions] looked at me and said, 'What makes you think you can be a graphic designer?' I was so upset, I went home, threw a fit, and didn't go back for a year."

But Michele couldn't support her kids on a secretary's salary. "I knew I had to do something. I was scared, but I was also desperate." Desperation, I've observed, is the principal reason people finally quit playing Not to Lose.

"I decided to stop feeling sorry for myself and make that interviewer eat her words," Michele said. "I went back to the school and said to the same woman, 'This is what I want to do. I'll answer any argument you give me with why your argument isn't valid.'" Spoken like a true champion who had at last gotten in the right game: To Win. Michele was granted admission on the spot.

RULE TWO: JUMP IN, READY OR NOT

There is only one way to join the high-earning game. You jump right in. You set your intention, let go of the ledge, and just start—anywhere. It really makes no difference where you begin as long as you're playing in the game To Win. Nor does it matter how gracefully you enter. Each woman I spoke to made the leap in her own unique way, some more calculated than others.

As you would expect, many of those with an M.B.A. under their belts jumped directly into high-paying jobs fresh out of college, often in big-ticket industries like investment banking or management consulting. Others started at the bottom in pay and position, then rose up through the ranks. Over the years, their salaries evolved along with their responsibilities.

Some of the women I interviewed were very methodical about their every move. Catherine Fredman, for instance, left *Working Woman* magazine to become a freelance writer, but instead of "going scattershot after any assignment, I figured out my strengths and I focused on specific areas that paid the highest: travel and business. I put out feelers and in six weeks I was swamped. I made six figures my first year."

Others leapfrogged from job to job. Bette Sussman built her career as a musician by working clubs, writing jingles, composing songs, just "being out there networking, meeting people. That's how your name gets around and how you get gigs."

Still others, like Michele Page, sprang into self-employment with one simple act: She put a business card on a public bulletin board. "Two days later I got a call from a publicist who needed a graphic designer. He fed me so much business for a year, I was working nonstop."

And surprisingly, a lot of women I interviewed literally stumbled onto the six-figure path without much forethought about which direction they wanted to go in. Berna Barshay, a literature major, had no idea what she wanted to do after graduation. She was clueless but intentional. "I just knew I wanted financial independence," she said. "I interviewed with every kind of business that recruited on campus. I ended up with a global financial firm, who actually hires a fair amount of liberal arts majors. I knew nothing about business or finance. I learned a lot, had a great time." She's since worked at a number of firms, including the hedge fund where she was when we spoke.

The real beauty of the game To Win is that you can begin playing anytime, ready or not. You don't need all the pieces in place or your route all mapped out. You don't need extensive training or formal education. In fact, you don't need to know much at all. You just need to get out and do something, anything. As one woman told me, "When I advise kids in their twenties, I say, 'When in doubt, act. Just do something. You can only sit, reflect, make lists for so long.'"

That's the line of thinking housewife Karen Sheridan followed at age thirty-nine. She didn't let a little thing like the lack of a college degree dampen her determination. She set out to find a job that paid $25,000, a lot of money back in 1980, particularly for someone with no experience. She put on her only suit, parked her car downtown at 10:00 A.M., and walked into the office building nearest the parking lot. "I went into every office on every floor and said, 'Hi, I'm Karen, and I'm looking for a job.' I got a lot of offers, but not at the amount I wanted." She continued this ritual for months. Finally, she recalled, "On the fourth interview with a lawyer, I said, 'I suggest you hire me today and pay me twenty-five thousand dollars.' He said, 'How about twenty-four thousand dollars.' I said, 'Close enough.'"

In the game To Win, it is perfectly OK, and highly encouraged, to shoot for the moon, to aim for the "unreasonable." I was amazed at first by how many brave souls dove headfirst into uncharted waters before they had any idea how to swim. Of course, sometimes they had to be pushed.

Eileen Michaels was one of those spunky women whose unexpected divorce became a kick in the pants. "I loved being a nurse, but I couldn't support my children on $136 a week," she told me. "I decided to go into a business where I'd have financial freedom. I called someone I knew in the brokerage business. I said, 'Hire me, send me to school, train me, teach me how to be a broker.' I didn't know anything about money."

When I commented on her courage, she shrugged it off as no big deal. "I didn't think it was such a strange thing. I didn't know anything about medicine before I went to nursing school. Money was just another language I needed to learn."

I heard this same message over and over: *It doesn't matter how much you know, it only matters that you're willing to learn.* That was Karen Sheridan's approach. After working at the law firm for a few years, she intentionally found jobs in fields she knew nothing about, like accounting, banking, investing, even retail. "From the moment I got any job, I studied, read, learned everything I could. I'd have one- or two-foot piles of paper stacked in front of me and I'd read every single piece about that company. I immersed myself in it. I was a sponge."

Andi Bernstein had recently begun working at a cable network and Internet firm after a nine-year hiatus raising her kids. "I knew hardly anything about computers. They weren't a big part of my past working life," she told me. "I just took a deep breath and jumped. Half the battle was learning all the new terminology. I listened. I went to every meeting. I taught myself as much as I could. I talked to people. Everything became an opportunity to learn. This job helped me realize that I have skills I didn't even know I had."

Jumping in cold can be very scary, as most of my interviewees will attest. It's especially disconcerting at the very beginning, when you're not quite sure what you're doing. That's the way the learning curve always feels at first, as if you're in over your head. Unfortunately, a lot of people bail out before they realize how close they are to taking the prize. The women I interviewed may have been tempted but they never backed down. They felt the fear and stayed the course. (There it is again!) And they strictly adhered to rule three.

RULE THREE: KEEP ON TRUCKIN'

When Harriett Simon Salinger jumped into her new venture as an executive coach after going broke in her seminar business, she was sixty years old and scared to death. But rather than cave in to the fear, she plunged into the work. "My intention was to have a successful coaching business," she told me. "I didn't plan it out. I had no idea what it would look like. I just rolled up my sleeves, got in the game, and began to retool myself. I completed a coaching training program, joined the chamber of commerce, attended networking groups, taught lots of classes. One thing led to another. I started getting referrals and it gelled."

Persistence is a prerequisite in the game To Win. Once you jump in, you've got to keep swimming. There is no doubt in my mind, after doing these interviews, that an ounce of talent and a pound of persistence make anything possible. One thing always leads to another.

Gerri, a successful freelance writer, would agree. "There are a lot more talented writers than me not making a decent living," she told me. When I asked the key to her success, she responded by paraphrasing Peter DeVries, " 'I only write when I'm inspired, and I make sure I'm inspired every morning at nine A.M.' " Plus, she added, "I'm tenacious. If someone doesn't like a story idea, I'll come back with something else."

Financial adviser Eileen Michaels is also bound and determined. "There was no such thing as 'feel like' when I was building my business. I worked whether I wanted to or not. I made an agreement with myself that so much would get done every day. I was committed to doing whatever I had to do. There were lots of times when the markets were down and my colleagues would leave. I'd say, 'Today is the day I need to call everyone.' "

Six-figure women seem to know without thinking that this rule of persistence has to be strictly enforced. "I did whatever it took" is what all of them said.

They put in long hours, especially at the outset, volunteered for unsexy assignments, signed up for extra training, accepted any public speaking opportunity that came along, returned every phone call, got involved in community organizations, networked, made friends with reporters so they got quoted in the paper, stuffed envelopes. They did whatever it took whether they felt like it or not.

"And then," they would say, "the money began coming in."

One word of caution is necessary here. I've watched too many underearners wear themselves out with nothing to show for it. Unless you have a profit motive, all your hard work may never pay off. I had a writer friend recently complain, "I've worked so hard my whole career. If only I'd made money my priority, I would've found something that rewarded my talents with money, not just pretty words. But I've been living in this ivory tower of literature, where monetary concerns were positively embarrassing, crude, and vulgar."

However, when you play by the rule of persistence, and you're playing with an intent to make money, hard work eventually bears fruit. "You just have to have the faith that if you keep putting yourself out there it will happen," said graphic artist Michele Page. "I was relentless. I never said no to anything. I never judged a job as too small, too big, or too wacko, as long as I could live with it morally. I made lots of sales calls. Whenever I met someone I always would say, 'Guess what I do.' Lots of times they didn't know what a graphic designer was, so I'd tell them and by the time I was done, they'd want to hire me. People just started calling. It was word of mouth, and the word spread."

Observing this rule is particularly important in the early phases of employment and also during any downturns or delays. Many of these high earners' career paths took some erratic and capricious turns. All sorts of unforeseeable events, from ill health to industry slumps, could easily have knocked them off the game board. There were some who became sidetracked, but by sticking it out, they managed to stay in the six-figure game. Or as one woman said, "It was just a matter of getting out of bed every morning and saying I'm going to do the best that I can."

Debbie Reynolds, once a glamorous star, had to rebuild her career several times after a series of setbacks. "It was luck at the beginning," she said, still gorgeous at sixty-eight. "But after the studio system changed, it became sweat and hard work. You had to go on auditions with thousands of other women. Then after my bankruptcy, I hit the road, working tents, toilets, any job anywhere, just trying to rise above the crisis. It's a hardship doing one-nighters, traveling across the country. You can't think any job is too small . . . just get a job."

Playing To Win can be exhilarating and at the same time humbling and exhausting. What enables six-figure women to keep plugging away tirelessly? They attribute their remarkable persistence to a six-figure secret: They love what they do. "I love the creative process. I love working with the people," said graphic artist Michele Page. "My greatest pleasure is helping my clients," financial adviser Eileen Michaels told me. "When you do what you're passionate about, everything falls into place," echoed Gerri, the writer. "I was passionate about the company so that gave me lots of energy to do it," Andi Bernstein said about her cable and Internet firm.

RULE FOUR: GRAB OPPORTUNITIES

You begin the game To Win by jumping in. You play it by persevering. And you triumph by grabbing opportunities, or, even better, by creating opportunities yourself. Every woman I spoke to was a classic example of this rule in action.

Patricia Cloherty, the highest earner I interviewed, was a Peace Corps volunteer who happened to meet someone forming a venture capital company. "I had no idea what that was," she said, laughing, "But I liked the idea of starting companies." They've been partners now for years.

Ruth Vitale, a former advertising executive, was at the '21' Club when a business associate introduced her to the second in command at Time Warner. "He called the next day and offered me a job," she said. She jumped at the chance, kept seizing opportunities, and is now copresident of Paramount Classics.

Many people confuse the opportunity rule with luck or fate, and then bemoan the lack of it in their lives. But really, luck itself has little bearing. It was their determination, not destiny, that made all the difference.

"I never looked for a job, things just fell into place. I've been very fortunate," said Sharon Whiteley, a sort of renaissance woman who has managed a number of businesses, from real estate to consumer products. But in the next breath, she clarified for me, "'Good fortune' is different than luck. Good fortune is being blessed with smarts that when something beneficial crosses my path I take advantage of it, whatever it is."

As often happens in the game To Win, Sharon's initial opportunity came from out of the blue. "I was working as an account executive in advertising and one of our clients who developed shopping centers thought I'd be right for his company. I said, 'Why not?' It was an exciting challenge and they offered me a lot more money. This opened the door to a whole new career."

I can't tell you how many of these women's success stories started out with a lucky break. The truth is, everyone's life is full of happenstance. The "lucky" ones realize that in every synchronicity lies potential opportunity and are quick to capitalize on chance occurrences. Of course, it's one thing to spot an auspicious event, quite another to follow through. Luck takes courage. High earners are willing to go where underearners fear to tread.

"People say I'm lucky," makeup artist Kris Evans told me. "You can be lucky once, but you have to be prepared to grab on to an opportunity and run with it." Her opportunity came when Barbara Walters's makeup artist called in sick and Kris was asked to sub. "I wasn't a fabulous makeup artist when I started with Barbara. I was so nervous, I left my keys in the cab so I couldn't get in my house that night. But they liked me. I stayed with her for two years."

This opportunity rule puts success within reach of all of us, even when all the odds are stacked against us. It explains why so many women I interviewed hit pay dirt in the most unlikely places, women you'd never predict would do so well. I can't think of a better example than Dianne Bennett.

"I was destined for the trailer park, honey," she told me in her husky voice. "I quit school at twelve, had three kids by the time I was seventeen. I was doomed. I passed a civil service test by one point and lied about my age. I'm no rocket scientist, believe me. I began as a Beverly Hills meter maid.

"Of course, everybody's nice to the meter maid or you'll get a ticket," she said, laughing. "So I met rich people and became friends with them. I'd introduce them—entertainment attorneys to screenwriters, but mostly men to women. I could see what I was doing in private could be a business, a big business. There are a lot of rich singles. There is money in matchmaking, and I am good at it. So I said, 'Let's go for it full blast.' I took out an ad, got a call from a client, charged him five thousand dollars, and found him a wife. I advertised some more, joined organizations, went on talk shows. It all just happened." Today, Dianne's fees as a professional match-maker start in the tens of thousands.

These examples may look like "it all just happened." But, believe me, that was never the case. The women I spoke to were relentless and resourceful in their search for opportunity. Sheila Brooks, for example, got thirty-three rejections for an entry-level job in radio and television. "Everyone told me, 'Sheila, you know you can't start in a major TV market like Seattle. It just doesn't happen.' But I kept going back and applying. Finally, I went to a TV station and said to the woman who interviewed me, 'Look, you've got to give me an opportunity. Let me volunteer.'" Six months later, that volunteer placement turned into a full-time position, which eventually led to a high-profile job as an anchor and reporter.

Admittedly, not every successful woman grabbed opportunity with equal gusto. What counts in this game is that you stay in the game, cashing in on coincidences, regardless of how anxious, pessimistic, or unenthusiastic you feel. Victoria Bullis, an aspiring career psychic, was told repeatedly that she'd never make money doing readings. One day a friend who was an agent for rock stars persuaded Victoria to appear on a radio show. "I didn't want to do it," she told me. "She had to come to my house, pick me up, and drive me to the studio. I was so nervous." Despite her stage fright, the show was a success, and the host invited Victoria back the following week. That night, sixty people called requesting appointments. She set her fees at $400 for forty-five minutes. And she's effectively used radio ever since as a major source of clients.

RULE FIVE: NO EXCUSES ALLOWED

In the game of six figures, excuses are to earnings what doughnuts are to dieters—strictly forbidden, or they'll be your undoing. If you fail to comply with this rule, it will knock you out of the game faster than any pink slip or bad economy ever will.

Many of the six-figure women I spoke to were prone to excuses when they first started out. Barbara Blair told me, "When people encouraged me to go into sales, I said, 'I can't go into a big office with a big man sitting behind a big desk.' It was very intimidating."

But her intention outweighed her intimidation. Even though she was shy, introverted, and insecure, she'd try to psych herself up with positive thoughts. "My parents didn't think I could do anything. I was raised to be taken care of," she said. "So I'd brainwash myself. I'd get up every day and say, 'You're going to make it. It's hard to do. It's much easier to sit in a slump. But you can't let the fear stop you.' Sometimes it stops me a bit. Then I have to talk to myself. You just have to say, 'This is how I have to think, just for this hour.'"

Some of the women I interviewed had valid explanations for why they couldn't succeed. In fact, every one of us can make a perfectly logical and convincing argument why we shouldn't play this game, follow these rules, or even attempt to make six figures. The true test of a six-figure woman is her refusal to buy into these pretexts. Excuses are cop-outs. They're smoke screens. They have only one purpose—to keep fear and trepidation at bay. Saying "I can't" is just another way of saying "I'm afraid."

Much of the six-figure game is played in our heads. We can only go as far as our beliefs will allow. As Karen Sheridan told me, "If you believe in yourself, a college degree is immaterial." Listening to these women's stories lent enormous credence to the old saw "Belief creates reality." Here's how the best players gain an edge: They concentrate more on what they need to do rather than what they hope to avoid. They play the game To Win the way it's supposed to be played, putting in maximum effort despite the possible hazards.

That's how Andi Bernstein described her successful foray into the cable and Internet world. "I didn't focus on skills I lacked. I didn't start thinking about all the more qualified people they could have hired. I just said, 'I can do this. I may have to work really, really hard. But I will just do it.'"

"You can't listen to 'There's not a lot of work' or 'There's too much competition,'" said makeup artist Kris Evans. "If I bought into that I'd still be in Cincinnati with six kids and working at a grocery store."

RULE SIX: IGNORE NAYSAYERS

No matter what you intend to do, there will always be someone to throw cold water on your plans. If you want to keep playing To Win, the rule is, as one wit said, "Let the dogs bark." Naysayers are part of the game. Whatever happens, don't let them stop you.

Right after art school, Michele Page, then age thirty-eight, took a six-month internship. "One day the president of the firm stopped me in the hall and said, 'I hate to say this, but you are way too old to make it in this business. Graphic design is a young person's business. You'll be an old lady before you'll make a decent living.' He didn't mean to be mean. He really believed it. I heard that from other people, too. It was a good thing he said it to me. It made me so angry it motivated me to prove I could make it."

Michele was right. Naysayers are not necessarily mean-spirited. They simply come with the territory. My theory is that whenever we dare to do something different, some benevolent cosmic being sends a whole bunch of people to tell us what a dumb idea it is. These people actually perform a valuable service. They come to test our level of commitment. If you notice, the more tentative you feel, the more pessimistic they sound. If they succeed in discouraging you, be grateful. You didn't have the moxie to make it in the first place. This is good information to have. It means you need to go back and tune up your intention or let go of what's holding you back. On the other hand, if you're determined to succeed in spite of these killjoys, then you most certainly will.

Among the high earners I met, there wasn't one who hadn't encountered her share of naysayers. Perhaps the most dramatic example was Gail Cave, who had no education and a violent husband who demanded she stay home with the kids. Yet she dreamed of being a dentist. "People looked at me like I was crazy. Everyone said, 'How are you going to raise two kids and go to school?' They gave me every reason not to do it. Even my dentist told me not to. But once I got it in my head, I knew I'd find a way." And she did.

RULE SEVEN: NEVER PERSONALIZE

Criticism and rejection are unavoidable in the six-figure game. If you're playing To Win, you can't take them personally. Or as Sheila Brooks put it, "I realized that people would be shooting all these emotional arrows at me so I had to develop the skin of a rhino and let them bounce off."

Thick skin isn't normally considered a female trait. Every woman I interviewed developed this rule the same way a baby learns to avoid a hot stove, through repeated experiences. In this game, as in life, enlightenment is often preceded by pain.

Early in her career, financial adviser Eileen Michaels was in a meeting with a man who made a rude remark to her. She turned to him and said, "That was really insulting. You hurt my feelings." He went, "Yeah? Get over it."

"You know, he was right," Eileen said. "I chose to be in their game. Can you imagine going to a football game and saying to the players, 'I want to play but don't tackle so hard.' Once you're in the game, and you agree to play you can't think you're going to change it. My business is a tough business."

All business is tough. And as you climb higher, the stakes get bigger, the game gets tougher.

Karen Sheridan was working at a large corporation when she was promoted to vice president, which, she said, "was hugely prestigious because there were very few VP positions. That was the good news. The bad news was that they all hated me. I got beat up so bad in that job. It was real cutthroat."

"How did you survive?" I asked her, wondering if I could.

"I realized I couldn't take it personally," she explained. "I think people get into more trouble because we personalize stuff. We think other people's criticism is about us. When people criticize me they're just giving me information, their personal opinion. These guys didn't know me well enough to not like me. They may not have liked the fact that I reported to the CEO and they reported to the senior VPs. But that had nothing to do with me personally."

Faced with hostility or opposition, these successful women found ways to cope. Each one I spoke with had discovered, in her own unique way, what politician Adlai Stevenson told us years ago: "Pain is inevitable. Suffering is optional." They could easily have personalized the remarks, found fault with themselves, let the pain fester. Instead, they deflected critical remarks by summoning their inner reserves, reading motivational books, talking to a counselor or friends, doing what Sheila Brooks called "changing my perspective."

"I had to make myself believe that rejection was just what I needed to succeed," Sheila explained. "I made up my mind that the more rejection I was willing to handle, the more successful I would be. I learned to use it to my advantage."

Women whose jobs mattered deeply to them both professionally and personally felt particularly vulnerable and exposed when dealing with criticism. Graphic artist Michele Page explained it this way: "You're showing your soft spot to the world. If the world comes back and says we don't value your work, it's painful, very painful. And it's very difficult to continue to put yourself out there. But I keep doing it."

The solution for Michele, and many others like her, has been to focus on a higher purpose instead of immediate gratification. Passion and purpose are powerful motivators.

Michele puts her ego on hold by reminding herself why she wanted to be an artist. "People have told me I take criticism so well. I tell them, the reason I'm here is to take your vision and use my experience to come up with a successful product that helps you achieve your goals. I'd rather people think of me as a phenomenal collaborator than a phenomenal artist."

Consultant Carol Anderson felt the same way about her specialty in gender diversity. "This is something that really matters to me," she said. "When I walk into a room full of men and women, I'm scared I don't have the tools to help them see another way of relating to each other, scared I don't know enough, scared that the men are going to get angry. So I go in assuming that we all have a real longing to create a better world. When I forget that I get scared because I think I'm alone here, rather than part of a shared consciousness."

It's fascinating how big a difference a mental turnaround can make, which proves an important point. The game is, after all, only a game. And games, we all know, should be fun. But when they're not, when your work becomes demoralizing, disheartening, or destructive, then, as the song instructs, you need to know when to walk away and know when to run. It's one thing not to take criticism to heart and quite another to tolerate abuse.

Gail Sturm told me she took her first job in commercial real estate "having no idea what I was getting into. I was working with seventeen men, none of them wanting me there. They tried to sabotage me. They'd send me on wild-goose chases. They'd flirt with me, harass me. I finally left and went to another firm. There I became extremely successful."

When a corporate culture is blatantly unhealthy, the best thing we can do is leave for someplace more supportive. And that's what many women I interviewed eventually did, the majority following a national trend, opting out of the corporate world altogether. Some left because of maltreatment, others became fed up with big business. "I was just so frustrated with the politics," Sheila Brooks told me of her final days in TV news. "I called up my husband one day and said, 'I'm going to quit and start my own business.' He said, 'When?' I said, 'Today.'"

And indeed, that day, ten years ago, Sheila began the game all over again, but this time, on her own terms.

THE RULES RECAPPED

1. Decide which game to play.
2. Jump in, ready or not.
3. Keep on truckin'.

4. Grab opportunities.

5. No excuses allowed.

6. Ignore naysayers.

7. Never personalize.

Once you're in the game and you've got a handle on the rules, understanding the next two strategies is how you'll ultimately take home the trophy.

7

STRATEGY #4:
SPEAK UP

God gives food to every bird, but does not throw it in the nest.
—NEW ENGLAND PROVERB

Women need to say to the world:
"This is what I'm good at. This is what I can
do for you. This is what I'm worth."
—PATTI WILSON, CAREER COUNSELOR

About five years ago, marketing manager Kim Finnerty, age thirty-six, made a disturbing discovery. Everyone at her level was earning more money than she was. Actually, this was nothing new for Kim. In other jobs, whenever she'd complain about being underpaid, she'd always hear some rule why they couldn't give her more. "You are too young for that much of a raise" or "We only give four-percent increases."

"I'd go along with that or quit," she told me. But this time was different. She liked the firm and didn't want to leave, so her only alternative was to "steel myself up" and talk to her boss.

"For the first time in my life, I spoke up for myself," Kim admitted. "I told him I was contributing as much as these other people and I knew they were making more. He said, 'Yeah, you're right. We'll have to fix that.'" Kim stood there in shock.

"I expected more of a fight. I thought he'd tell me I was crazy or he'd say, 'Oh no, we can't give raises in the middle of the year.' I was surprised that it was relatively easy. He raised me to just over $105,000, which got me on an upward spiral. The other folks working at my level were making more like $160,000, so in the next few years, in a couple of good-sized steps, and big bonuses, he got me up to that level and beyond. It went very fast from there," she said, then after a short pause added, *"I wish I had screwed up my courage a whole lot earlier."*

I heard this same rueful observation from virtually all the women who were slow to hit the six-figure mark. Call it the Lament of the Latecomers. Their greatest regret was their reluctance to speak up. I could almost hear each one slap the side of her head for not realizing this sooner.

"If only I had spoken up, negotiated a promotion—instead of trusting management to do the right thing," a longtime employee of a large corporation told me.

"The reason I didn't make six figures immediately," said a business owner, "is because I didn't ask for what I was really worth. I underpriced myself."

"Knowing what I know now, I should have said something sooner," groaned a woman who had spent fourteen years in a partnership where she brought in most of the business but only got a portion of the profits. "I let myself be taken advantage of."

Each of these women eventually recognized, as Kim finally did, an undeniable truth about the way the world works: *If there's something you want, you've got to speak up.* This strategy is based on the principal tenet of higher earnings: If you don't ask, you don't get. "You are never going to get what you deserve," explained one astute woman. "You are going to get what you demand." Like it or not, your financial fate depends heavily on what you're willing to ask for, no matter how stellar your conduct, how vast your experience, or how impressive your credentials.

"I've always rested on my credibility and performance," said Linda Giering, a former Dupont employee, whose six-figure salary was late in coming. "But I've learned that's not what gets you ahead in life."

"What does it take?" I asked.

"Chutzpah," she said, laughing. "I never really fought for money. I was shy about asking for raises and promotions and things like that, which in retrospect is the wrong approach. And I could never say no. That's part of the reason I didn't get to where I wanted to be. I was always overcommitted. It's taken me a long time to say no, to stand up for what I believe and negotiate for what I want. I could have been making a lot more today if I had."

THE CONSEQUENCES AND REWARDS

Lack of "chutzpah," perhaps more than anything else, explains why the wage gap persists and the glass ceiling is still intact. It explains why management recruiter Lester Korn told a reporter that women had become "managerial bargains" in executive searches. And why Julie Adair King, the author of *Smart Women's Guide to Interviewing and Salary Negotiation*, declared, "If we don't get the jobs for which we're well qualified, if we don't earn the salary we deserve, it's sometimes our fault."

It's our fault because when, instead of asking for the salary we want or the promotion we desire, we acquiesce, we go along with the program, often resorting to two strategies that are common practice among underearners. One is to silently stew. The other is to pack up and leave, only to meet the same fate somewhere else. Either way, the outcome is the same—a lifetime of lower pay.

Few people consider the long-term consequences of this kind of compliance. Every concession you make compounds over time. When you accept 75 cents for every dollar a man makes, you'll lose up to $250,000 over your lifetime. And as sociologist Lois Haignere figured out, a woman whose starting salary is only $1,000 less than a man's will lose more than $84,000 over forty years when both receive pay raises of 3.5 percent annually.

And it's not just money you lose. When you fail to speak up, you turn into a victim. And victims are easily exploited. "Either control your destiny or someone else will," I once heard a speaker say. Anytime you don't say what you need, feel, or think, you forfeit control. The good news is, it's never too late to take back control. The moment you do, your whole life can change. When you speak out instead of clamming up, you'll not only make more money but also create more balance, achieve your goals, and win the respect of others.

Teri Cavanagh, a bank executive, was exhausted from the constant pressure and long hours of her job. "Coworkers were having heart attacks and strokes at age forty. Why did I think this wouldn't happen to me?" she asked rhetorically. "I threatened to quit but waffled every time. The money became a big trap. I felt powerless."

Then she discovered that the same strategy she used to increase her salary could be used to lower her stress.

"I started empowering myself by speaking up, saying what I wanted and setting boundaries."

For instance, during a recent vacation, she was summoned back to her office for a big merger meeting. "I said no, I am still on vacation for two more days. They said OK, when I got back I could meet with the executive vice president instead." Two days later, the VP kept her waiting twenty minutes for their appointment. "I finally said to the secretary, 'If he's not here in five minutes I'm leaving.' He showed up.

"This was new for me. I expected the corporation to be more considerate. It was hard to be that insistent." But when we say what we want, and say it with conviction, as hard as it may be, it usually gets people's attention . . . and admiration.

Jenna Graham used the same strategy after she was promoted to vice president of perhaps the most prestigious laboratories for basic and applied research in the world.

"When the men heard they would report to me, they freaked out. I was the only woman, I didn't have a Ph.D., and who did I think I was? Of course, I wanted to cry because they hadn't given me a chance. But in our very first meeting I went in and said, 'I heard you don't want me to be your boss.' Dead silence. Then I said, 'Look, either you're going to work with me or against me. If you're going to work against me, I'm going to fail and you're going to fail.' By the end of the meeting, I'd won them over." Then she added quietly, "I was shaking in my pants!"

GOOD GIRLS DON'T

Perhaps of all the strategies mentioned in this book, speaking up is the toughest for women, who are less confident and have lower expectations in negotiations than men. According to one study, even women who display the same negotiation behavior as men feel less successful than men do ("Gender and Conflict Resolution and Negotiation: What the Literature Tells Us," by Ira G. Parghi and Bianca Murphy [www.ksg.harvard.edu]). Why are women so hesitant to assert themselves? And why do they still feel dubious after they do?

In part, it's the way we were raised. As girls, few of us were encouraged to speak our mind, so we have trouble doing so when we're older. I remember in group one day, a comment from an under-earner prompted every head in the room to nod in agreement. "When I grew up I was told 'Be a good girl, don't speak unless spoken to, and never contradict.' You were supposed to recede into the wallpaper. I think that's why it's really difficult for me to feel comfortable promoting myself."

You're not likely to find much reinforcement for speaking up from the present-day culture, either. According to the *Journal of Social Issues*, women with a "directive style" are evaluated more harshly than men. "Competent self-promoting women risk being disliked and rejected, especially by men," concluded the authors. Likewise, in studies by the Management Research Group out of Portland, Maine, men got high marks from their bosses when they were forceful and assertive, but women were downgraded for displaying the same qualities. To be quite candid, the double standard is alive and kicking—assertive men are respected, assertive women are resented. And the women I interviewed said as much.

"I sometimes feel, in meetings, that being direct and straightforward is interpreted as bitchy, whereas from a man it would just be forceful. It's intimidating," a senior vice president reported.

Being cast as a bitch when they're acting confident and bold has even subdued some of the highest earners. Women by nature are relationship-driven. As much as we hate to admit it, our need to be liked and our fear of rejection will often inhibit us from taking a stand. What a pity. Trying to please everyone is always a formula for failure.

Another formula for failure is to assume that others should recognize our talent and know what we want. Way too many women hold this belief. Consequently, they don't ask for what they want, or they resent having to do so. I vividly remember insurance company executive Brooke O'Shay telling me how angry she was that she had to ask her boss for the promotion that finally put her into six figures. "It took a long time for me to get to a point where I wasn't mad he wouldn't say on his own, 'You deserve it.'" With that kind of thinking, as Brooke will attest, we are the ones holding ourselves back by keeping ourselves victims.

THE <u>REAL</u> REASON GOOD GIRLS DON'T

These explanations are but the tiniest tip of a much deeper, more insidious problem. When I asked Kim, whom we met at the beginning of the chapter, why she didn't speak up earlier, her response captured the real reason women have trouble with this formidable strategy. "I always question whether I am worth that much," she admitted. Ask any underearner why she hasn't asked for more, and you're likely to hear the same thing. Underlying our unwillingness to speak up is a woman's own inclination to devalue herself. "The enemy isn't men," the author Betty Friedan once told an audience of workingwomen. "The real enemy is women's denigration of themselves."

Until we learn to value ourselves, we'll have a hard time pursuing this strategy. The most salient point about speaking up, as I learned from my interviews, is that you have to consciously and deliberately recognize your worth . . . and make sure others do, too.

When you have a sense of your worth, higher salaries seem to follow suit, simply because you're more inclined to make sure they do. But without that certitude, that belief in your own value, you lack the "oomph," the fervor, to take a strong stand. In our interview, Ingrid, a six-figure psychologist, told me she had recently helped two different clients, a man and a woman, negotiate six-figure contracts. "He had no trouble," Ingrid observed. "But she immediately started questioning herself: 'Am I worth it?'"

This kind of self-depreciation goes right to the heart of our financial ruts. To become a six-figure woman, we must speak up cogently and convincingly, bargain hard without becoming hard, and stand firm when we're feeling shaky. Sure, negotiation techniques and assertiveness skills can easily be learned by taking courses or reading books. But the truth is, if you're going to command more—whether it's a higher fee, more flexible hours, or a corner office—you have to truly believe you're worth it. People will always respond far more to your "vibes" than your words. Or, as Emerson once put it, "Who you are speaks so loudly I can't hear what you're saying."

"If you don't believe you deserve a certain fee for your services, then the person requiring your services isn't going to believe it," noted musician Bette Sussman. "If I'm working with a celebrity, which I am now, I go in there saying, 'This is what I need. This is my fee. If you want me to go to Los Angeles, this is how much I need to travel.' A lot of people are afraid to stand up for what they want because they're afraid to lose the gig. You can't be afraid."

Bette's right. You can't be afraid. But what if you are? A startling number of six-figure women admitted they were skittish about speaking up. Face it, if it weren't so scary we'd probably all have more zeros on our paychecks and more balance in our lives.

"As self-confident as I am, asking for what I think I'm worth has been a huge problem for me," declared a successful business owner. And another longtime high earner said, "I keep waiting for it to be easy, but it never is." Even a seasoned executive almost sheepishly confessed, "Sometimes I've asked for more, sometimes I haven't. It's hard. It's hard for a lot of people. I don't know if it's women only, but it certainly is hard for the women I know." And another told me that whenever she goes to ask for more, "I hear voices in my head saying, 'Who do you think you are? No one will pay that.' Once the voices quiet down, I can do it."

You may never completely silence the voices that question your value. But that doesn't mean you have to listen to them. The challenge for each and every one of us is to keep raising the threshold of what we'll accept *in spite of* the unnerving racket of negative chatter that keeps playing in our brains like a broken record. The question is how?

SELF-WORTH = NET WORTH

These women developed their chutzpah like weight lifters build muscle, by continually pushing themselves to take a stand, ask for more, demand what they're worth, and say no when appropriate— despite their trepidation. Applying this strategy always entails asking for more than feels comfortable. This is crucial to bear in mind. Remember, the ability to tolerate discomfort is a requirement for raising the bar. For many of us, that requires nothing short of a paradigm shift.

"I knew, deep down, two things," PR consultant Beth Chapman told me. "You have to think you're worthy of better money, and you have to ask for it. But there is a whole part of you that dissociates from what you're worth. Once you get beyond that, then the sky is the limit."

How did Beth come to realize her worth? How did the others? I asked that question and listened carefully to the answers. What I learned is that within even the most insecure of us is the innate knowledge of our inherent value. It may be only a glimmer, it may be deeply buried, but it's there. Your job is to find it, fortify it, then let the world know how valuable you are and that you expect to be compensated accordingly. Here are some suggestions I learned from these women for pumping up their self-worth along with their net worth.

RAISE YOUR FEES

For many, like Beth, discovering their value was a matter of following their dreams. They simply get in the game, stay in the game, give it their all, and do their very best. With each small achievement, each tiny victory, they gain a greater sense of their own merit.

"I think I crossed that value barrier about four years into the business," Beth acknowledged. "Before that I was still trying to justify my retainer fees on how many hours I worked. Then one day I got a client on the front page of the *Wall Street Journal* and you could hear his enthusiasm a mile away. I think at that point I began to realize just how valuable I could be."

With that realization, Beth began raising her price, but even then it wasn't easy. "I would talk to myself in the mirror and try to say those fees without laughing. Getting it from my brain to my mouth is nine-tenths of the work."

Then one day, when two people Beth didn't want as clients asked her rate, she doubled it. "They both said yes. I suddenly realized how *vastly* underpriced I was. So the next time I had new clients ask my price, I doubled it again. And I kept doubling it until I started losing clients."

THINK BIG, THEN EVEN BIGGER

Inspired by my interviews with women like Beth, I started following the example of other entrepreneurs who had set their fees inappropriately low. They'd test the limits of what they could charge, ratcheting up their prices little by little to see what would happen. Nine times out of ten they got what they asked for. Looking back, many of them, myself included, had the same reaction and came to the same conclusion Carol Anderson did:

"One of my objectives was to make more money working less time. So I started this experiment of raising my rates five hundred or a thousand dollars for each new project. People gave it to me without blinking an eye. It was such an insight. It made me realize that I didn't know how to think big enough."

That's really the work most of us must do, entrepreneurs and employees alike. *Think big. And then keep thinking bigger and bigger.* What most of us do is unwittingly limit our earnings by lowering our expectations. "I can't tell you how many women I've had sit across from my desk and say, 'I got this perfect job but I sold myself down the river,'" Berkeley, California, career counselor Patti Wilson told me in exasperation.

Even in studies where women are trained in negotiation strategies, they set their sights lower and end up with less money than men. As one venture capitalist told *Business Week* (March 9, 2000): "Usually a guy will shoot for the moon and know it's unrealistic . . . in hopes that he gets what he needs. Women, on the other hand, don't ask for enough money to accomplish what they want. They're much more conservative." Granted, grandiosity can work against you, but women are too inclined to go to the opposite extreme. The idea is to value yourself fairly compared with others in your field or at your level.

DO YOUR HOMEWORK

One of the worst negotiating mistakes women told me they made was picking a number "out of the air" and finding out later it was way too low. The smarter ones do their homework to avoid that pitfall. They found out their market value by researching the going rates.

Traci Des Jardins negotiated a six-figure salary in her first job as an executive chef even though women chefs were blatantly underpaid. "When I negotiated that job," she told me, "I looked around and tried to figure out what was appropriate in terms of compensation. Not just for women but for men. If you don't learn the market value of what you do, you can easily be taken advantage of."

How do you find this information? In magazines, on the Internet, in the want ads, from trade associations, employment agencies, headhunters, and colleagues. (See Resources, page 259.)

For example, Internet consultant Kitty Reeve struck up a frank conversation about fees with another consultant during a meeting of Women in Multimedia 40+. "She told me she had started at seventy-five dollars an hour and with every new job she went up five dollars an hour so that she was now making ninety-five dollars an hour. That had never occurred to me. And I had no idea that some people make ninety-five dollars an hour for what I was doing." This discussion marked Kitty's entry into six-figure territory.

Brooke O'Shay finally entered six figures in her forties, when she was assigned the workload of two departing managers with no increase in pay. "I've always taken what's been handed me rather than saying this is what I want," she told me. She found another manager who was doing the exact same job but was two levels higher. That conversation, Brooke said, "gave me a lot more sense of where I was, comparatively speaking, for the work I was doing. I saw I wasn't being compensated adequately. That more than anything gave me the confidence to say, 'I'm already doing more than I should be doing at this level. So if you need me to do more, I need a promotion.'" To her amazement, her boss agreed.

"Initially it was very difficult for me to ask. But when it was done, I understood I had to be personally responsible for my compensation." As we all do!

GO FOR MORE

Every job has a salary range. The rule of thumb is to aim for the upper end of the curve. Get as much as you can *up front* by asking for more than is offered so you have room to maneuver. It's a basic ploy in negotiation: Negotiate down, never up. In the six-figure game, this ploy is part of the protocol. According to a recent poll by the Society for Human Resource Management, more than 80 percent of the HR professionals said they expect counteroffers. Teri Cavanagh learned this from a coach she hired to help her negotiate her starting salary with the bank that made her an offer.

"This woman told me you only get one chance and you have to ask for a hundred thousand dollars because then you're in a different category. You're underpricing yourself if you ask for less." For Teri, who had barely made twelve thousand dollars the prior year trying to salvage a fledgling business, getting those numbers out of her mouth took more nerve than she thought she had.

"The interviewer asked me what would meet my expectations. I heard my coach's voice say, 'You only have one shot.' I heard myself say, 'I think I'm worth $110K.' I heard him gulp. I said, 'It's really what I need to see.' He said, 'Fine,' and I said, 'Wow.' Then he said, 'What if we pay you $100K and make $10K a signing bonus?' I knew enough to get it into base pay—that's how they calculate bonuses. I said, 'No, I want $110K.' He gave it to me."

LOOK BEYOND SALARY

Whenever you negotiate for more, think beyond base pay and more toward a whole package. As most women told me, it's not necessarily salary that gets you to six figures. The real game, said a corporate type, is making bonuses and being on the right projects.

"There are ways of negotiating contracts where you can get things that are not literally money in your pocket, but in essence are," TV anchor Rikki Klieman explained. The list of negotiable benefits is endless: bonuses, stock options, vacation time, commuting expenses, flextime, and early salary review, to name a few.

When Rikki negotiated her contract with Court TV, she told the person she was dealing with exactly what she needed. "I gave them a number of points having to do with money, expenses, the status of a particular show, and the hours I would work. The advantage of having several items is you always have one or two that you can give up. If you just go in and say, 'I need X dollars,' then you have a problem."

(This negotiation strategy has been called the salami technique. Asking for slices of the salami, instead of the whole thing, increases the likelihood both parties will feel they've made a good deal.)

Of course, some things are more negotiable than others. There are instances when the pay is fixed, the benefits are standard, and there's no room for haggling, period. But six-figure women still give it their best shot. As freelance writer Anita Saville discovered, "Sometimes there is some wiggle room and sometimes there isn't." The key is to be creative. For example, when an editor seems inflexible, Anita will say, "'OK, I'll take it at a dollar a word this time, but if you like what I do, you'll have to give me my standard rate the next time.' Or sometimes I'll ask to split the difference, so you're giving them a deal without giving away the store."

ACT AS IF YOU'RE WORTH IT

Asking for top dollar takes a lot of spunk, which most of us won't feel at the time. But just because you don't feel it doesn't mean you can't fake it. As we've seen, even six-figure women have doubted their worth, but to all the world, they appear undaunted. Chef Traci Des Jardins understood this very well when she asked for six figures. "I decided on a certain level of compensation, asked somewhere above that, and negotiated down from there. I got just what I wanted," she said quite matter-of-factly.

"You sound so confident," I remarked. "Did you have that much bravado at the time?"

She laughed. "Of course not! But I had to act like I did." Acting as if is, without a doubt, a surefire antidote for weak knees, a pounding heart, or a deflated ego.

A friend who calls herself a "recovering underearner" once read me a caption in a magazine under a Tom Cruise photo: "Yeah, they pay me a lot to make movies, but I'm worth it."

Those last three words became her reference point. "I'm going to act like that, even though lots of times I don't believe it," my friend proclaimed. The next time I saw her, I wasn't surprised when she told me, "You know what? I'm starting to believe it!" When you act as if you're worth a lot, you'll eventually convince yourself as well as others.

"If I were to pass along my experience to other women," Anita Saville told me, "I'd say, 'Act as if there's no room for argument.' I mean, when I say, 'This is my standard rate,' I try to say it like, 'Of course, this is what I should get.' The more confident you act, the more likely you are to get what you ask for."

"I never waffle," a consultant agreed. "If you communicate with authority, you'll always get more. That's one of the reasons I'm getting such high fees."

EMBRACE YOUR "BITCH"

"You have to be tough in order to be heard," Kris Evans pointed out. "I try to be diplomatic and fair, but I'm very direct so it's unmistakable what I'm asking for. I spent the first three weeks on my first job being low-key and quiet, and nothing got done."

The surest way to get what you want is to be direct, self-assured, and candid. But here's the rub. When you do speak your mind, you're often labeled a bitch! Which, contrary to popular opinion, is *not* a bad thing. There's tremendous strength to be found in our "bitch." She's our "warrior." My friend Carol Duffy likes to say "bitch" means Being in Total Control of Herself. Instead of biting our tongue for fear of sounding too tough and risking rejection, we need to embrace our bitch, that forthright part of ourselves who is willing to walk through fire to make her voice heard, who will fight for her rights as fervently as a lioness protecting her cubs.

Beth Chapman, who was unexpectedly fired from her corporate position, took that opportunity to toughen up. "They wanted me to bow out like a nice little lady," she said. "Well, I didn't. I got an attorney and challenged them on the firing because it was no cause. I won a big lump sum and a full year's severance, which allowed me to start my own business."

Financial adviser Heidi Robertson, who was raised by a strict disciplinarian father, found it painfully difficult to be confrontational. But when three male colleagues were promoted over her, she got angry enough to confront her manager head-on. "Something is not right here," she insisted, after storming into his office. "I'm better than all three of them. This is the last time I'm going to be passed over." And she stormed back out. Two months later, she was promoted. Still, she admitted, "It was a hard conversation to have."

Talking tough, embracing your bitch, does not, by any stretch, mean compromising your femininity, though several women have made this mistake. I had a very moving interview with a senior executive, the only female at her level. "I overcompensated and started acting like a man," she admitted, her voice laced with pain. "I went in demanding respect, always wore black, and adopted this tough-chick persona. It felt fine until I wanted to be loved by a certain man, and he considered me one of the guys rather than a desirable woman." She has spent this past year "rearing the feminine side of me. I realized this persona didn't do anything for me. I thought that's what I needed in order to be respected. Now I walk in as an adult woman, not a tough chick. I even wear pink. I rely on my abilities, not an act, and I get the respect."

TAKE THE INITIATIVE

You can offset a tendency to downplay your achievements or counter lowball offers by having tangible evidence of what you bring to the table.

"Point out your value to the company," insisted publishing executive Sally Wood. "Maybe you saved X amount of dollars or had an idea that generated so many sales for the company. Whatever job you're in, have a file at home where you keep a tally of everything you're doing for your company. Walk in with that at review time."

Many smart women offered the same advice. Taking the initiative is an effective means of demonstrating your value and your intentions to the organization.

"Don't wait for the annual performance appraisal to find out how you're doing. Be proactive," urged Valerie Gerard of *Smart Money* magazine. "Go in and ask for work, ask for responsibility, ask for challenge. Ask your manager for an assignment that will make his or her life easier. Let them know if there are openings that interest you."

This is exactly how women I interviewed broke through the glass ceiling. They let the powers that be know exactly where their sights were set. When Roberta was sent to an executive program outside the office, she let her boss know she expected it to go hand in hand with a move forward in her career. "I told him I hoped it would lead to greener pastures, and it did. I was the first woman in this office to be promoted to officer level."

Similarly, when after fifteen years on the financial end of the business, Julia, an oil company executive, wanted a line job, she had no qualms about speaking up. "I was very open about it. I told my boss and people in the operating company what I wanted. I became the first woman and the first financial person who has ever been in this position." And she added, "In my last three out of four jobs, I had approached the person when the job opened and said, 'I'm really interested in that job. You should consider me.'"

NO IS NOT ALWAYS NO

The women I interviewed didn't let statements like "This is all we can give you" or "That's not possible" discourage them from asking for more. The truth is, as Brooke O'Shay discovered after petitioning for her promotion, "everything is up for negotiation. People will say, "We don't do that," but that's a bunch of bull. Just because it's not standard operating procedure, it's still possible."

One woman told me she was to be transferred to Chicago, but she wanted Los Angeles, where her fiancé lived. The company told her it was out of the question. Did she let that stop her? "It took a lot of finessing to get L.A. It wasn't in their plans. But I persisted. I kept asking. Eventually they gave me what I wanted."

I spoke to another woman who had just returned from a six-month sabbatical, which was unheard-of at her firm. "Sometimes I'm amazed at the things I ask for and get," she remarked. "I assumed I wouldn't get paid while I was gone. But I consulted with a compensation expert and she said I should try to get fifty percent of my salary. I asked for seventy-five percent, thinking I'd negotiate down from there. But they approved it unanimously."

I think my favorite don't-take-no-for-an-answer story came from Jan Goldman. She was selling art supplies but had her heart set on becoming a broker for Merrill Lynch, which she considered the premier brokerage firm. Granted, she hated math, flunked the screening test, and they flatly rejected her application, but she was unwavering. "I wanted to work there so much, I fought my way in," she recalled. "I went to the branch manager's office before he showed up, sat in the chair in front of his desk, and waited. When he came in I said, 'I know I can do this.' That made all the difference. He hired me."

KNOW WHEN TO WALK

It takes chutzpah to speak up. It takes even more to walk away. One of the biggest differences between high earners and their lower-paid peers is the height of their breaking points, the minimum they'll accept, the place at which they'll shake their head no. "I might knock off a thousand dollars if someone says they can't afford me," offers political consultant Cara Brown. "But I don't go down a lot. I'm worth what I do." Similarly, when makeup artist Kris Evans tells clients her fees, "if they say, 'That's too much,' I say, 'Thank you very much,' and I move on."

Technically, turning something down is a form of speaking up (just as it is a variation of letting go). When you walk away, you're saying to yourself, the other person, and the universe, "I am worth more, I deserve more, and there is more where that came from." And based on the stories these high earners told me, the universe, if not the other person, *always* responds favorably to those cues. Without exception, when a woman turned her back on one thing, something better came along.

Gayla Kraetsch Hartsough, a former teacher, learned this lesson when she applied for a job as a kindergarten aide. "I was twenty-two years old, sitting at this interview, and I said, 'How much does it pay?' He said three thousand dollars. And I said, 'That's part-time, right?' And he said, 'No, that's full-time.' I said, 'I couldn't work for

you for that. I work too hard. You'd be getting too good of a deal.'"
She turned around and walked away. "Two months later, he called
and hired me at six thousand four hundred dollars. I left after four
years, making eighteen thousand dollars."

Rosa Hernandez also enjoyed a big jump, parlaying a $200,000
offer into a $400,000 deal.

"How did you do it?" I asked in awe.

"I told them that I was worth more, that I had another job offer,
and that I had to make a financially responsible decision. They said,
'OK, we'll get back to you.'" She left the room doubtful that her
demands would be met, but sure enough, "they came back with four
hundred thousand."

An alternative to walking away is shutting up or adopting what
one writer called the "Hmmm" response. (Instead of replying yes or
no to an offer, simply nod thoughtfully and say "Hmmm." "The
'Hmmm' response can drop another ten grand in the bank for high-
level executives," claims Jack Chapman, author of *Negotiating Your
Salary: How to Make $1000 a Minute*.) Not only is silence an effec-
tive negotiating strategy, but, ironically, it can be a very potent way
of speaking up. "I've learned that silence is often mistaken for wisdom," observed Ruth Harenchar, an accounting firm executive. "I'm
a very outgoing person, but I've learned that there are times when
nodding sagely and sitting quietly is a very good maneuver."

MORE THAN MONEY

Speaking up as a strategy has ramifications that go far beyond
money, however. It works like this: Asking for more is an act of *self-
love*. Saying no is a show of *self-respect*. Refusing to settle is a statement of *self-worth*. And walking away is a sign of *self-trust*.

Whenever you stand up for what you want, whenever you refuse to take less than you deserve, you reinforce your self-love, self-respect, self-worth, and self-trust. In time, you'll begin to notice a shift in how you feel about yourself. Speaking up becomes not something you *should* do, but something you *have* to do—because you know in your heart you're worth it.

8

STRATEGY #5:
THE STRETCH

*I've not ceased being fearful. I've gone ahead despite
the pounding in my heart that says: turn back,
turn back, you'll die if you go too far.*
—ERICA JONG

Success is the child of audacity.
—BENJAMIN DISRAELI

The philosopher Søren Kierkegaard once declared, "To dare is to
lose one's footing momentarily; to not dare is to lose one's self."
Those words could well be the credo for today's six-figure women.
High earners are keenly aware of the immense power of audacity,
which comes from the Latin word *audace,* meaning to dare. The
women I interviewed somehow intuitively (if not always eagerly)
embrace this strategy as common practice: *Stretch, dare to do that
which you think you cannot.*

Every one of us, at various times in our lives, has had to make
that choice: stick with what's doable or take the more demanding
route. For a six-figure woman, the decision is a no-brainer.
Without exception, each one came to a situation where her first
reaction was "I can't do that" and then, powered by her intention,

she went on to do it—not just once, but over and over again. Basically, this is how the game is played: Go as far as you can, then stretch even further.

Early in our conversation, political strategist Cara Brown quoted a line from an Alanis Morissette song: "I recommend biting off more than you can chew." "I say that to myself all the time. 'Don't sell yourself short, stretch yourself,'" she explained. "There have been lots of times where I've had a great opportunity and I thought it was way too much, but I did it anyway."

Audacity is the leitmotiv of the six-figure formula, the recurring note that echoes through every strategy mentioned so far. Declaring a lofty intention can be quite a stretch, as is letting go of the ledges that make us feel safe. It certainly takes guts to get in the game, just as it requires chutzpah to speak up for oneself. So what's different here?

This particular strategy, while implicit in the others, requires a particular kind of daring—a stretch beyond what's comfortable to the seemingly impossible. Typically, it's preceded by the thought, I can't do that, and occurs at pivotal points in a person's career. It's as if each call to stretch was an initiation of sorts, as if each act of daring became a private rite of passage. The audacity to do what felt intimidating, if not out of the question, was precisely what pushed these women to the next level—often in earnings, usually in skills, always in self-esteem.

Just as significant, any mention of audacity was conspicuously absent from conversations with underearners. I would often ask women in my groups if, in the course of their careers, they'd done something they thought they couldn't do. Their responses were pretty much like Marta's: "Offhand I can't think of anything. I guess I worry I won't do it good enough."

A WAY OF LIFE

When I asked six-figure women the same question, their typical comeback was, "All the time!" "I scare myself to death every day," one woman said, chuckling. "I think if you are not doing that, what's the fun?" exclaimed another. Psychologist Rollo May would say of these women, "They take the cards that make them anxious." Indeed, high earners challenge themselves to stretch like Jane Fonda goes for the burn.

"It's how I live my life," declared financial adviser Victoria Collins. "I always get myself in situations beyond my ability and rise to them. I've driven home saying, 'Where is your brain? You don't know how to do this.'" That's how she came to write her latest book, *Investing Beyond .Com.* "I knew nothing about the Internet when the publisher asked me to write it, but I was passionate about learning."

"In my experience," explained self-employed author and consultant Karen Page, "the most successful people feel the fear and do it anyway. It's a matter of not being intimidated by the fear."

Karen learned the value of this lesson in her first job after business school. She was part of a team scheduled to make an important presentation to a London-based client. No one else was available to travel, however, so she had to go on her own.

"It was a huge task, typically taken on by someone who'd been at the firm for at least five years. And I was there for maybe six months," Karen recalled. "It was very intimidating. I had never made a presentation on my own before. I had never been to Europe. I didn't even have a passport. Traveling that far, doing the presentation, representing my firm, every aspect terrified me. But I never let that show. I just went ahead and did it."

Not only was the presentation a success, but Karen was promoted faster than anyone else in the firm. That kind of audacity, she asserted, "has stood me in good stead over the course of my career."

From that day forward, Karen adopted what I have observed is the classic six-figure stance: *If it's not illegal or immoral, find a way to get it done.*

"Everybody can say no, can give you a million reasons why something is impossible, why it can't be done," Karen noted. "But I think whatever you're asked to do, you do it. It doesn't matter how scared you are or if you don't know how to do it. You say yes and take responsibility for getting it done."

In fact, just prior to our interview, Karen had gotten a call from a client with an absurd assignment—to write a business plan in forty-eight hours. "I knew it was impossible. He knew it was impossible. And I said yes." She barely slept, but she got it done right on time. "That plan was hugely successful in raising fifty million dollars for the firm. And it made me a lot of money."

The whole of this strategy can be reduced to three words. *Just say yes!* Whether it's to your heart's desire or your boss's request. Go for it. So what if you don't know what you're doing. The quickest way to become a high earner is not to wait until all bases are covered or for opportunities to fall at your feet, but to go out and consciously seek them.

I was genuinely moved in my interview with hedge-fund manager Renee Haugerud, when she quoted a statement from *The Road Less Traveled,* by Scott Peck: "Dare to be God." "I tell that to every young woman I meet. Dare to be God. Dare to be all you can be. Dare to make a decision, even if it's wrong. Dare to make something of your life, even if you fail." Then, after pausing briefly, she added, "We need to keep success and failure in perspective. As Rudyard Kipling said:

'When you meet triumph and failure, treat them alike, as the imposters they both are.'"

BOUNCING BACK

As Renee suggests, not all daring acts are resounding successes. A leap of faith implies a loss of footing. There will be occasions when, instead of landing on your feet, you'll fall flat on your face. The true measure of success is not what happens but how you react to what happens. In the six-figure sector, resilience is as important as audacity.

Three years ago, Katie Cotton's boss at Apple Computer offered her the directorship of corporate communication. The new position meant a jump into six figures and a major jump in responsibility. "I'd be going from managing five people to managing twenty-two people," she told me. "My first reaction was, I'm not sure I can do this. I was a hotshot PR practitioner, a big fish in a little pond. I was really good at what I did. Could I manage a team of people and drive a larger effort? I wasn't sure I could. Why take the risk and fail?"

At the same time, she thought, What if I take the risk and I'm successful? And then, Wouldn't I regret not trying? Katie opted to take the plunge.

The first months on the new job were frightening, demanding, and thoroughly demoralizing. "I wasn't a very good manager," she readily admitted. "I made a lot of mistakes. I wasn't as patient as I should have been. I didn't invest enough time helping get people on the right path. You know, all those pretty basic management 101 things."

But as other six-figure women do, Katie stayed in the game, learned the ropes, recovered her bearings, and eventually reaped the rewards. During our interview, she could barely contain her enthusiasm for her job. "I love what I do. It's not just the money. I love managing a fairly large team, and we produce amazing results. I feel successful, absolutely."

There's only one way to reach those higher returns: You go as far as you can, then stretch even further, and when you fall down, you pick yourself up and keep right on going. *The resilience to bounce back from defeat and disappointment is what distinguishes a stellar success from the run-of-the-mill.*

"If I've learned anything about getting stronger," Olympic figure skater Nancy Kerrigan once remarked, "it's that you can listen to only one voice—the one that says, 'Get up.'" And, she might have added, the other voice that says, "Go for it . . . again."

So often, however, our determination gets drowned out by the voices of doubt, the ones that wonder, What if I can't? But, as Shakespeare warns us, we mustn't let our doubts become traitors. Those questioning voices are there for a reason. They're instinctive attempts, albeit misguided, at self-protection. As much as you may want financial success, who likes the idea of possibly screwing up? Stepping outside your comfort zone, doing what you think you can't, means risking embarrassment, humiliation, rejection, or disapproval.

FINDING THE GIFT IN THE GAFFE

None of the women I interviewed saw failure as fatal or irreversible, at least not for very long. Even though it hurt to lose a bid or botch up a project, these six-figure women used the experience to their advantage, looking for lessons rather than brooding over losses. In fact, many of them told me that what they learned when things went wrong was so important that they felt they received far more than they lost.

I could almost hear Donalda Cormier, a consultant, cringe when she described to me over the phone the first time she taught negotiating skills. "I was terrible, really terrible. I remember reading the evaluations and crying. They were brutal." But she also knew they were true. She had done her best, now she had to learn to do better. "I didn't like it, but I fixed it. I never made those same mistakes again."

Think of your own life. Haven't your most valuable lessons come from your most trying experiences? Hard times, like heavy weights, build muscle. I observed, among the women I interviewed, that the most audacious were those who had endured the most adversity, especially as children. Interestingly, the other early influence on high levels of audacity as an adult was athletics. Many women who appeared inherently daring had played sports as kids, often, though not always, competing with boys.

Audacity not only requires courage but also augments courage. Every leap of faith prepares us for bigger things down the road.

"Believe me, I wasn't born with the gene," exclaimed entrepreneur Mary Helen Gillespie. "It was through confronting my fear of failure."

She points to her quantitative analysis class in business school as a prime example. "It was so difficult it was painful. For years the math thing prevented me from getting an M.B.A. But I did it anyway. I stared it down, living it, breathing it, crying over it, and walking through it. That was the lesson I needed to learn. Not so much how to do regression analysis, but the fact that I could marshal all my forces and get through the class, that I could do this no matter what."

Every memory of a hard-won achievement becomes a testimony to what's actually possible. Precious milestones for the psyche, these memories can be easily evoked to stimulate our flagging self-confidence. As one woman who single-handedly built an Internet site told me: "I often look back on that when I have tough things to accomplish and I think, If I could do that, I can do anything."

Most of us don't realize how capable we are until we have an opportunity to surpass ourselves. Each time these women stretched, even if it took repeated attempts to pass muster, when they finally pulled it off with flying colors their belief in themselves shot up several notches. And for this, they were tremendously grateful.

As Karen Page pointed out, "It's easy when you're fearful to become negative and think things won't work out. But if you look back and see how things have worked out over the course of your life, there is overwhelming gratitude. And there's hope—if it worked out in the past, it's likely to work out in the future—so you keep plugging."

BEYOND THE BULL'S-EYE

Headhunter Susan Bishop used a wonderful analogy for making a stretch—a target with a bull's-eye.

"That dot in the middle is your comfort zone," explained Susan. "The things you do day in and day out; you've done them for years and you're comfortable doing them."

The next two circles surrounding the bull's-eye represent the learning zone. "You're a little uncomfortable, not completely sure of yourself, but it's where you're going to learn the most.

"And the outermost ring is your danger zone, where you won't be able to learn because you're too far away from where your core abilities are."

The way you reach the six-figure range is by putting yourself in extraordinary things. This was the worst setback ever, but I know I have it in me to get up and do it again." And that's exactly what this six-figure woman did.

But first, she said, "I had to stop blaming myself, going 'Oh God! I am a failure.'" She began looking at what she really wanted. And as a result, her life actually got better than ever before. "I was forced to reevaluate. I was never happy managing huge sales forces so I cut my doll business back to a much smaller scale. This allowed me to start coaching and speaking, which is really where my heart is right now. I picked myself up and went right back out there."

THE TRAP

A word of warning: "You have to be brave enough to take risks and shrewd enough to avoid those that are too big," Dr. Sheri Wren, CEO of one of the largest female-owned businesses, told the *New York Times* (May 10, 1998). In other words, *bite off more than you can chew, but not so much you choke*. The trick to stretching without snapping is to challenge yourself on this side of what's reasonable, to take what various women referred to as "prudent leaps," "well-reasoned chances," "manageable risks." Failure is inevitable, but if you find you're having more than your share, it's time to reassess your game plan. You may have stretched yourself too thin. However, for most women, that's usually not the issue. It isn't that they're taking too big a risk. It's that they're either too hard on themselves, extremely impatient, or overly meticulous.

Less than a year ago, Suzanne, a longtime member of the six-figure club, had joined a start-up technology firm. From the very first day, she saw she was in over her head. But instead of cutting herself some slack, she pushed herself harder.

the learning zone about 30 percent of the time: by making tough decisions, accepting difficult projects, attending meetings with people more advanced, participating on committees you know little about, assuming a leadership role, relocating to a strange city, speaking in public, doing whatever you must, whether you feel like it or not.

Over time, you'll find yourself saying, "This isn't so hard. I can do this. What was I afraid of?" The learning zone will become your comfort zone. And then it's time to push yourself into the next ring of learning. You must keep enlarging the circle, increasing your skills, testing your confidence. To stop stretching is to stagnate.

"After I got over being scared and nauseated and thinking I was going to look absolutely foolish, it astounded me how much I really did know," Kitty Stuart told me, referring to the early days of her vintage Barbie doll business. A former actress and grade-school dropout, Kitty was freshly divorced and hanging by a financial thread when she turned a hobby into a livelihood. She knew nothing about running a company. But as she discovered, "if you have the nerve to get out there and go for it, you know more than you think you do, and you are going to be pretty successful. You just have to force yourself to push yourself."

Simply put, that's how this strategy works. You force yourself out of your comfort zone and then force yourself back up when you take a tumble. Kitty has done both. Just as sales were beginning to skyrocket, her business came to a shuddering halt. A huge robbery pushed her into bankruptcy.

"I really thought my life was over. I had worked so hard. I just wanted to drop dead. I just thought, OK. You can drop dead now or get up and face this thing head-on."

It took a while for her to regroup. She went through a terrible depression, until she got mad. "I thought, Damn! I've done some

Women, in general, tend to react like Suzanne. The most unreasonable demands we encounter are those we inflict on ourselves. Harboring excessive expectations is like walking on land mines. You never know when they'll blow up in your face or wreak havoc on your career. Six-figure women are an ambitious bunch. This trait accounts for their remarkable achievements, but it can be their downfall when taken to the extreme. When they set impossible standards, they run the chance of going into a panic and slipping into paralysis.

Even Suzanne admitted that she, not her boss, kept turning up the heat. "He knew I had no tech expertise when he hired me. I was setting these superman expectations for myself," she told me. The harder she pushed, the more ineffective she became. "I was really a mess for a couple of weeks. I was crying a lot, I couldn't concentrate. I wasn't eating. There was literally no way I could work."

The high level of stress Suzanne suffered triggered a chemical depression, not uncommon among hard-driven overachievers. Some solve the problem by finding another, more appropriate job. But for die-hard overachievers, quitting usually isn't the answer. The same thing is likely to happen in the next job as well. The best solution is to learn to lighten up. Suzanne went into therapy, got medication for the depression, took a couple of weeks off, and then returned to work with more realistic goals and a much better attitude. The last we talked, she sounded vastly improved. "I'm actually having fun," she told me.

Undue pressure, even if self-imposed, is bound to backfire—either by rendering you ineffective or by keeping you tethered to safety, unwilling to stretch. Underearners are particularly vulnerable. I remember when a friend, Stacy Ferratti, a corporate trainer, once confided to me over lunch why she had never made six figures. "I know, to make this kind of money, I have to be willing to put myself out there," she said. "But I have these really high standards that are impossible to meet. I always feel I have to be perfect. What if I screw up? What if someone sees I don't really know what I'm doing?"

Her course of action had always been to play it safe. As we talked, however, I observed a shift in her thinking that would eventually turn her into a six-figure woman. "You know, if I screw up, I won't be the first person on the planet to do that," she mused, more to herself than to me. "I'll get through it. I'll learn from it and I'll make it right." Before a year had passed, Stacy broke through the earnings barrier by deliberately changing the messages she was giving herself. As she told me later, "I just keep telling myself I really am good at what I do. I really do have something to offer."

GETTING STARTED

Stretching makes only one demand: You must take action. After you say yes (or after you get back up), you must do something, anything, in spite of your apprehension. One woman called it the walk over hot coals. "You don't talk yourself out of something because it might hurt. You start walking and see how far you can go," she told me. Or, as they say in twelve-step programs, "'Do the action and the feeling will follow,'" another woman said. "I'm convinced you don't get over the anxiety and then take the action. You can't wait around to feel good. You take the action and the feeling follows."

Action is powerful. But there were times when even the most intrepid women had second thoughts. In those moments, the comfort zone looked awfully appealing, and they questioned their ability, not to mention their sanity, for wanting to leave it. But leave it they did, which is in fact how they came to be six-figure women (and continued to stay six-figure women). However, they have some suggestions for getting started when you feel stumped or discouraged.

• *Do just a little bit more.*

St. Francis of Assisi had some great advice for venturing into the discomfort zone: "Start by doing what's necessary, then what's possible, and suddenly you're doing the impossible." As many women discovered, the best way to reach success or recover from a slip can be by taking small steps at a slow but consistent pace. "I took it hour by hour, day by day," said Kitty Stuart about recouping from the robbery. "I just chipped away at something every single day. I'd pick up the phone and go, 'Guess what I am going to do now?' Once I'd told somebody, I'd have to do it."

Lucy Tomassi, a bank senior vice president, approached her whole career like this: "I'd start with what I knew, then I'd try to expand into something a little bigger." For example, as she grew more confident in her first job as a credit analyst, she devised a program to manage cash flow. "It was a natural outgrowth of what I knew I could do. Success really breeds success. When you start feeling like 'I can do this. I know what I am doing,' you start to perform better and people see you as more valuable."

It's a self-perpetuating cycle that keeps spiraling upward exponentially. Each little step outside your comfort zone adds immeasurably to your sense of self and others' assessment of you, which continually emboldens you to stretch even further.

• *Turn inward.*

But sometimes taking the tiniest step is like trudging through molasses. A part of you wants to forge ahead, but a bigger part would rather curl up in a ball. Well, action doesn't always have to be directed outward. Sometimes the best thing you can do is turn inward. And that's what many women I interviewed did. They took time to reflect, to consider the risks, rewards, and worst-case scenarios.

"When I want to undertake some new project, but I'm afraid," said business owner Barbara Doran, "I'll sit with a notepad and address my fears one by one. When I do that, I often discover they're not reasonable. It helps me push through."

Years ago, Susan Davis was considering leaving her senior position at an important bank to start a national nonprofit women's network. Everyone thought she was nuts. She was beginning to believe them. "I was forty years old. My kids were young. My husband was sick. And no one had heard of national networks or how you could make money from them."

Then one day, she recalled, "I went to the bedroom in the back of the house and lay down. When I thought about my risk, my whole body started shaking. I felt overwhelmed with fear and I let myself feel it. I stayed there until I was done feeling terrified."

She got up, resigned from the bank, and formed the Committee of 200, a powerful group of the country's top female business owners that has been featured in *Time* and numerous national magazines. The move propelled Susan's next career in the investment management field beyond anything she could have imagined.

There's a lot to be said for feeling the fear, I mean *really* feeling it, sitting alone in the dark with the monsters of your imagination, trembling to their invectives about what'll go wrong, letting them jab, scoff, rail, howl, and cast aspersions, until they finally hush up. Looking fear in the face is like throwing water on fire. Eventually the intensity will dissipate, the fear will run out of steam, and you can finally move on.

Joline Godfrey, a self-described "good corporate woman," had been with Polaroid ten years when she came up with an idea for a new business that became so successful it was spun off. She had a choice: "Take it and run or stay with a company I knew and loved." For one week, she'd go home to her backyard, cry, drink scotch, and wonder why in the world she'd trade the security of a steady paycheck for the uncertainty of self-employment. "I never thought I had an entrepreneurial bone in my body," she said. "But after a week, I put the scotch away and started a new company." Four years later, she sold the company and started another, which became Independent Means, a thriving organization that teaches girls about business.

- *Start anywhere.*

My friend Stacy swears there's a direct connection between her spike in salary and her success on a strict diet cutting out all dairy, wheat, and sugar. "I saw I could count on myself to stick to this diet, which I've never been able to do before and certainly not for this length of time. I started taking myself more seriously, especially at work."

A stretch in any area of life, regardless of where, has a ripple effect in other areas as well. If you can't quite get yourself to volunteer for that tough assignment, try signing up for art class or running a marathon, anything that puts you out of your comfort zone. Quite a few women credited experiential retreats, like Outward Bound, for making them more daring.

"I've done rope courses and jumped off of telephone poles and things like that where you think, Man, I can't do that. But then you do it," said one woman. "You come back realizing you have the ability to do ten times more than you thought when you just put your mind to it."

• *Stop and say thanks.*

I remember, a long time ago, a friend telling me that whenever she got scared or in a tight place, she would stop and feel gratitude for all that she had. "It changes everything," she explained. I would be hearing that reaction expressed repeatedly in my interviews. Many women told me they were actually thankful for their challenges, admitting they might never have succeeded unless they were pushed. And their gratitude gave them a much-needed perspective.

Marketing consultant Tracey Scott put it like this: "I feel grateful for all my experiences, even the bad ones." Like Tracey, these six-figure women were fully aware of a direct correlation between obstacles they had hurdled and their level of confidence. They all knew that without that belief in themselves, they'd never have gone as far as they had—they might not have even tried. "The people who get out of their comfort zone," Susan Bishop told me, "are the people who have the confidence to do what it takes, not once but over and over again."

The women I spoke to not only considered their challenges an asset but also appreciated *themselves* for tackling them head-on. "Every time I have to make a speech, I break out in a cold sweat," said an entrepreneur, "but I also give myself credit for being so brave."

The power of gratitude derives from a universal law: You draw to yourself whatever you dwell on. Or as Native Americans used to say, "Give thanks for unknown blessings already on their way." If you focus on all that can go wrong, don't be surprised if everything does. If instead you make a deliberate effort when life hands you lemons to find the blessings in the batch of bitter fruit, imagine how your attitudes will change, and your reality with it. If you appreciate what you have, you can't at the same time resent what you don't. A simple thank-you turns your attention from problems to possibilities. Many six-figure women had come to this same conclusion.

I talked to a woman who had lost out on a $4 million deal she had worked on for years. "I can run around having a total chip on my shoulder or I can take the blessings I've been given—my accomplishments have been amazing—and go from there." Which is what she did.

TAKING THE STRETCH

In life, as in fairy tales, the treasure always lies just beyond safety, and only the daring ever attempt the journey. The brave souls who do, these six-figure women, are the ones who bring back the proverbial pot of gold. Their fortune lies not just in greater sums of money but in something considerably more valuable: a grander vision of who they are. Each woman I interviewed recounted some form of this tale, and it usually sounded like this:

"I hate to sound egotistical," an entrepreneur said with sincerity, "but I truly believe I can do anything I put my mind to. I didn't become like this overnight. All those tough experiences made me who I am."

So the next time you find yourself saying, "No way I can do that!" smile knowingly. You are that much closer to becoming a splendid, audacious, six-figure woman.

9

STRATEGY #6:
SEEK SUPPORT

Every blade of grass has an angel that bends
over it and whispers: Grow! Grow!
—TALMUD

Hasten to that which supports.
—I CHING

Success is not a solitary journey. Ask any six-figure woman. They constantly spoke of the significance of other people to their financial success. They credited their families, friends, bosses, and colleagues. They emphasized the importance of informal networks, formal support groups, and influential connections.

At first, I understood this strategy to be about networking, making contacts, and finding mentors, but as I studied my interviews I saw that six-figure women have two specific types of support that underearners seemed to lack—*True Believers*, people who recognize their potential and offer encouragement, and *Way Showers*, people who provide the map and serve as proof that success is possible. True Believers say, "Go for it. You can do it." Way Showers say, "Let me show you how." Sometimes they are separate people. Sometimes one person plays both roles.

These two kinds of support do more than further your career.

They are both a stimulus and a supplement for all the other six-figure strategies. They inspire us to set our intention high and stick to it when our faith falls short. They gently pry our fingers loose when we cling too tightly to safety and then lead us into the game, explaining how to play. Maybe most important of all, they assuage our fears so we can stretch even farther.

As events planner Stephanie Astic put it, "Every time that little voice in me says, 'I think I've bit off more than I can chew,' I call my mom and she says, 'You can do it. What do you need?' That makes a huge difference. She walks me through the situation and the whole thing becomes so much easier."

Ideally, our parents are the first True Believers we encounter and, if we're lucky, they remain that way throughout our lives. In her study of twelve hundred successful women, psychologist Sylvia Rimm discovered that more than 98 percent had at least one parent who had set high expectations.

My research had a slightly different twist. Virtually all the women I spoke to knew someone who had grand designs for them at various stages in their lives, but that someone wasn't necessarily a parent. Actually, for every six-figure woman whose parents assured her she could be anything she wanted, there was another who grew up hearing she'd never amount to much. While parental encouragement is wonderful, it's not essential. What we miss in our youth can easily be made up for in later years. In fact, many told me that their abusive or absent parents had laid the groundwork for future success, giving them the courage, compassion, and resiliency necessary to achieve what they had as adults.

"I consider coming from a really difficult family of alcoholics a tremendous gift," one entrepreneur explained. "I know I can survive anything so I'm not afraid to fail."

Still, this woman and all the others found at least one person who wholeheartedly believed in their abilities, often before they fully believed in themselves, and offered them guidance by giving advice and/or setting an example. The combination of the roles, the True Believer and the Way Shower, inspirer and instructor, mentor and role model, created a synergy that fostered their aspirations, replenished their spirits, fueled their efforts, and bolstered their self-esteem despite snowballing doubts and endless hurdles. In fact, on the six-figure path, seeking support is not an option, but a requirement.

Many times a supportive alliance turns out to be a life-changing experience. That's how Nancy Lauterback, CEO of a speaker's bureau, described her first boss. "I went to work for him as a secretary and it changed my life. He was an esteem builder. He gave me the confidence I needed for the rest of my life. I watched him, absorbed everything. He guided me on how to be a better salesperson, that calling is the key to sales. He was a great role model."

ANGELS IN DISGUISE

Like angels from heaven, these significant supporters will often drop from the sky, at different times in your life, in an array of assorted disguises—as a teacher who recognizes your potential, as a relative who encourages your dreams, as a boss who challenges you to strive, or even as a stranger who plants a seed with a random comment.

For real estate broker Galina Blackman, a Russian immigrant, her angel was her grandmother, who had been imprisoned by the Communists. "After she was liberated, she dedicated her life to me. My grandmother is the reason for my success. When you're unconditionally loved, you can do anything. I never doubted I could become anything I chose to be."

Banker Lucy Tomassi found her True Believer in a high school teacher who persuaded her parents to send her to college. "No one in my family had even graduated from high school. When I wanted to go to college, my mother actually felt a sense of betrayal. But this teacher told my folks it would be a real shame if I didn't go. Her vote of confidence gave me confidence. I never wanted to disappoint her."

For lawyer Tracy Preston, that significant other was a supervisor she greatly admired. "No one had ever trusted me or believed in me like that before. She relied on me to do things I'd never done and because of those challenges I became more assertive, more willing to take on responsibility. She gave me the confidence I needed. Her faith in me had a lot to do with my becoming partner."

And senior vice president Nicole Young told me her True Believer was the mediator in her divorce. "He said to me, 'Someday you'll make more than your husband.' Yeah, right, I thought. My husband was a physician, making over $250,000. I didn't believe for a second I could ever make more than him. But I did. I made a lot more. That man, I truly believe, put it in my subconscious and made it possible."

True Believers and Way Showers frequently appear as if a gift from the gods, unannounced and unanticipated. But sometimes they don't. Sometimes you feel like you're all alone, with no help in sight. Fortunately, it's not necessary to idly wait for support to show up. You can go out and find it yourself. There were many times in the lives of the women I spoke to when they actively sought encouragement, handholding, and direction. But before we explore how to find more support, I need to issue a warning.

PITFALL NUMBER ONE

There are two ways in which a lot of us will have trouble employing this strategy. The first is our reluctance to ask for help. Too many women take pride in single-handedly managing the kids, their jobs, their house, an endless list of tasks. But excessive self-reliance breeds isolation, which can quickly erode self-assurance. Underearners are especially guilty. In my groups for underearners, I heard the same complaint innumerable times: "I've always felt like I have to do everything myself. I don't even imagine that there's help to be had or anyone would even want to support what I'm doing. That's why I've really appreciated this group. It lets me hear other stories, lets me not feel so alone, and I get feedback."

Six-figure women know what this underearner was just discovering—every Lone Ranger needs at least one Tonto. "I have learned to get on the phone and not feel guilty or bad or like I've failed if I have to ask someone for help," an executive told me. "I see it all the time at work—men will ask for help, women will try to cope."

Of course, sometimes high earners get themselves into a bind and completely out of balance when they start believing that no one else can do the job as well as them. Several admitted they had a hard time delegating, but the most successful, and sanest, women I interviewed eventually gave up trying to do everything themselves. They stuck with what they enjoyed most and did best, parceling out everything else, from cleaning the house to putting data on the computer.

"I always ask myself: Am I the only one who can do this? Or can I train someone and delegate?" explained a business owner who finally learned that "it's really OK not to be great at everything. Before, I'd try to do it all and then I had no time to do what I'm really good at."

PITFALL NUMBER TWO

The second way we can trip up is in failing to recognize or appreciate these angels of support when they do cross our paths. To benefit from support, you must be receptive. That means you have to consciously allow people who care into your world. And, equally important, you have to listen to what they say and take their words to heart.

I am convinced all of us have had many True Believers and Way Showers come into our lives, but too often we react like Allison, an underearner who admitted, "My parents told me a million times a day how great I was. I just never believed them," or Mary, who conceded, "People always say my art is great, that I should show it more often, but I'm suspicious of their sincerity."

Even high earners have had to overcome some initial skepticism. When the head of personnel called Lucy Tomassi into his office, she thought for sure he was going to fire her. "It was my mentality of I'm not good enough. But what he said was, 'Everyone thinks you're great. Have some confidence in yourself and you'll do fine.' He got me thinking. I started to realize how much those 'attaboys' really help you do better."

When we aren't willing to embrace offers of help or words of encouragement, because we either don't value ourselves or take our work seriously, then we virtually cut off the flow of abundance into our lives. You'll never reach financial success until you're willing to fully open yourself up to receive other people's support. Here's a hint: Even if you don't completely trust the praise, act as if you do. You have nothing to lose and so much to gain.

Financial services executive Nancy McGinnes put it this way: "If you surround yourself with people who support you and try to learn as much as you can from everyone you come in contact with, the only place for you to go is up a successful path."

"My business is not a solo thing," agreed CEO Charlotte Maure. "I have remarkable people supporting me all along the way. I think this is true of almost everyone who's successful. They find people who care about them, offer them advice and counsel, and help them."

Where are you most likely to find True Believers and Way Showers? In your significant other, your social network, your professional contacts, and your spiritual beliefs. While they are not all essential, the women who seemed to have the most balance and joy in their lives drew support from all four categories.

SPOUSAL SUPPORT

Psychologist Daniel Levinson, in his pioneering research on adult development, found that the number one factor for vocational success was forming "a system of relationships with other adults who will facilitate [one's] dream." The most important of these relationships, Levinson discovered, was a supportive spouse. Although Levinson studied only men, the same holds true for women. One of the most striking themes that emerged very early in my interviews among those who were married or in committed relationships was the central role a husband or a partner played in their careers. I never expected to hear so many women tell me, "If it wasn't for him, I couldn't have done it."

"The key is having a spouse who supports and encourages you and is your biggest fan," said investment adviser Victoria Collins. "My first husband put me down all the time, and it created so much self-doubt for me. But David is always telling me, 'You can do anything. I'm so proud of you.' I wouldn't be where I am today if not for his support."

The same held true for lesbian couples. "If she wasn't in my corner, it wouldn't have been possible for me to succeed," a businesswoman said about her partner. "The world is a tough place. Whenever I'm feeling inadequate or afraid, I talk to her. She doesn't know much about my business. It's more like having an ear and having someone to say 'go for it.' She gives me confidence."

The nourishing support from a spouse or a partner appears to be irreplaceable and irrefutably valuable. In fact, in a study of more than thirty thousand women in thirty-three countries, sponsored by Avon Products, a supportive spouse or partner was cited as the most important criterion for success in starting a business. These findings underscore how critical our choice of a mate is to our financial success, and that, yes, it is possible to find a man who is not threatened, but thrilled, by his wife's achievement. Here is a small sampling of what interviewees said when I inquired about their partners.

- "He delights in my success. He's never gotten in the way of our moving for advancement and never complained about my long hours."
- "He helps me with the kids and all their obligations. When I hit a pitfall, he'll talk me through it."
- "I have to say I have an amazing husband. He's the kindest, sweetest, most respectful, wonderful man, an incredible father."
- "He'd get up in the morning and travel with me and take the train home just so we could talk. When I came home and wanted to bitch and moan, he'd listen."
- "She's been right there for me, supporting me. With the two of us, we don't feel that there's anything we can't do."

- "He really takes time to review my financial statement and offer suggestions. He's just as concerned about my business as if it were his, even though it is one hundred percent mine."
- "I wouldn't have been able to do any of this without him. When I was in the midst of an M.B.A. program and starting my business, we were eating fish sticks and saltines for supper and he didn't complain. He simply was there and understood."
- "My husband was so encouraging. I know they say behind every successful man, there's a woman. Well, he is the great man behind me."
- "I would never have gone into business for myself if not for my husband. It was his urging and his support. He saw something in me I didn't see in myself."
- "He's so supportive, I can't even begin to describe it. I am not expected to put a cookie on the table or wash a sock. It's a true partnership."
- "He's a great dad. When I went back and got my degree, he took over with the kids."

BACKLASH!

"If a husband feels secure about himself, his wife's achievements can only add to a fulfilling relationship," declared *Psychology Today* (March 13, 1995). "But if a partner uses money as a power tool, they're in trouble." Sure enough, a number of women reported their success at work created trouble at home. One of the most painful challenges for some of these women was "spousal backlash." I asked

Lucy Tomassi—who, like most of the women I interviewed, earned significantly more than her husband—if her higher income had affected their marriage.

"It hasn't been wonderful for it," she confessed. "He's jealous, so he belittles me sometimes. Since he can't make more money than me, it makes him feel better to put me down."

"How do you deal with that?" I asked. Her answer: "I ignore it, or I suppress it."

If I were to lay odds, my guess is Lucy will eventually leave that relationship. Based on my interviews, if a husband wasn't supportive, the marriage usually didn't last. "It's difficult to have an unsupportive husband," observed the once-married Patricia Cloherty, a venture capitalist. "He didn't like my success. I'll never forget when I got a lifetime achievement award from my industry, and he was hell-bent on making it an unhappy event. I left him soon afterward."

When I asked how she kept from giving in to her husband's anger, she acted surprised I'd even ask such a question. But I asked because I saw so many women acquiesce when their partner got annoyed. I had done the same, and more than once. "I love what I do," she said emphatically. "It's me. To require I surrender my intellectual engagements was simply not acceptable. If I gave my work up I knew I'd die."

"Was it hard when he left?"

"There were some dark clouds for a period of time. Endings are hard. But the rest is liberating."

It's particularly difficult when the wife's career is on an upward trajectory and the husband's is headed down the tube. "I kept getting promoted and my ex kept getting laid off," Gina told me. "My success put a lot of stress on the relationship." She soon divorced. (However, as often happened, she later remarried a "wonderful man.")

I found this same negative reaction and hostile response existed in lesbian relationships as well. "Money and my success played a big part in our breakup," a high earner told me. "I was involved with a woman before I hit the six-figure mark. In the beginning we were equal. Then my income started to double hers. I felt guilty. She hated it. No matter how hard she worked, she'd still be making less. So she left."

Success and financial disparity don't have to break up a relationship. Especially nowadays when a high-earning wife is becoming more commonplace. In the 1980s, the economist Shirley Johnson calculated that for every $1,000 increase in a woman's salary, her chances for divorce increased by 2 percent (*Worth* magazine, June 1993). But recently, the *Washington Post* (February 27, 2000) reported that "marriages in which wives bring in more are not significantly more likely to end in divorce." A small number of women I interviewed weathered spousal backlash with their marriages intact. But it took a woman strong enough to stand firm, a partner mature enough to ride out the storm, and a couple willing to communicate freely and candidly. After all, *Psychology Today* noted, men weren't raised to share power and "they are confused about how to be supportive."

Heather's story proved to me that despite initial repercussions, two secure individuals can survive without sacrifice. By the second year of her marriage, Heather was making more than her husband and he was furious. "His anger was indirect and abusive. Finally, one night I said, 'You knew I was ambitious when you married me. I'm competing with myself, not you. If you don't like it, too bad. End of story. If this is a deal breaker, I've made my choice.' I felt good saying that. It took me a long time to work for what I had accomplished. I wasn't going to give it away."

Fortunately, she said, "I have a smart husband. He smoldered for a few days. Then a week later he said, 'I decided to give you a match for your money. You're not going to outearn me.' There was humor in his voice, but he meant business. The next couple of years it was a dead heat. I still make more, but it's just not an issue anymore."

"Were you ever afraid of losing him?" I asked. Her answer reflected the conclusion most six-figure women come to: The fear of abandoning themselves is greater than the risk of being abandoned by another.

"I could've lost him," she conceded. "It wasn't the money. It was the freedom to be me. When I look back on my other relationships, I've always subordinated my need for independence, but I've learned. I need to know I can stand on my own."

SOCIAL SUPPORT

If it's true that "a friend is a present you give yourself," then every day is Christmas for a high-powered woman. Each one I spoke with had the most amazing relationships with friends and family (men as well as women). Whether they connected through formal networks, family ties, or personal acquaintances, these associations blossomed into deeply personal, profoundly nourishing relationships that fed their soul and fortified their confidence, that nursed them through the darkest nights and paid tribute to their tiniest victories.

"My friends tell me how wonderful I am, and I really need to hear that," said Miriam, an investment manager. And events manager Sheila Milligan told me in our interview, "Just the other night, a friend and I talked about our struggles until two A.M. We both walked away feeling stronger."

Unlike men, who will talk to their buddies about everything from ball games to current events to avoid discussing their personal frustrations or exchanging emotional intimacies, six-figure women use their social networks to commiserate, complain, console, and celebrate. It's accepted that women are relationship oriented. It's less understood how relationships allow us a place to let off steam. According to the latest research, men and women react differently to stress. Men go into "fight or flight." Women more commonly "tend and befriend." "Engaging in being close to others has anti-anxiety effects for women," said *USA Today* (August 7, 2000). "It calms them down." I heard from everyone how camaraderie carried them through the most nerve-racking times.

Abby, who is single and self-supporting, not only has a demanding job as an attorney but also suffers from chronic fatigue syndrome, a debilitating illness.

"How do you do it?" I asked her with genuine admiration as she described the disabling exhaustion she endures on a daily basis.

Her answer was immediate. "There are days when I wish I could just stay in a fetal mode, but I plow ahead because I have the foundation of family and friends. I don't know how many times I've called my sisters on the phone and whined when things are going bad and I'm depressed. They help me get through whatever rough patch I'm in."

Likewise, when I asked Stephanie French, a single mom in a high-powered job, how she handles the pressure, she, too, didn't miss a beat. "I have wonderful, fabulous, incredible friends," she said. "I don't know what I'd do without them."

She gave me a typical example. "I'll have a day of political turmoil at the office, then I'll come home and the bills have to be paid, the kids are in a bad mood, and I'm just cracking from exhaustion, ready to slit my throat. But I'll pick up the phone, call a friend, and they'll listen, give me good advice, and then they'll start making me laugh. By the time we're through, I hang up, feeling fine."

WEEDING AND RECULTIVATING

This strategy is all about growing our support system. But it's also about pruning what gets in the way. Have you noticed that whenever we make changes, we're sure to upset someone close to us? Usually someone who's resisting moving forward themselves, whether it's a spouse, a parent, or a friend. One woman explained it to me this way: "I think a lot of people are used to you the way you are, and if they see you growing, they're threatened by it, and they want to keep you from becoming someone else."

To uphold our intention to increase our earnings, it's essential to be with people who will cheer us on, not try to rein us in. Too often I see underearners hanging out with pessimists, worrywarts, folks who are generally fearful. The only thing they're likely to support is the status quo. Six-figure women, on the other hand, are drawn to risk takers, or at the very least, to those who applaud their efforts to go out on a limb.

Just as many of the women I talked to had left difficult husbands, many also lost old friends, and did so deliberately.

"I did a lot of 'weeding out' of people I had known for many years," entrepreneur Kitty Stuart told me. "I was very careful not to be around people who made me feel bad about what I wanted to do. When I heard, 'You're in your forties. What in the world makes you think you can do that?' I just chose to stay away from those people. I cultivated a really strong, fantastic group of people who were supportive and also shared visionary ideas."

One popular way six-figure women cultivate new relationships with people of the same ilk is by joining support groups, which became, for the women I interviewed, intimate forums for bonding on a very deep level.

Miriam attends a monthly gathering of Harvard Business School female alums. Prior to the first meeting, she admitted, "I expected to see all these cold, unfeeling, successful women who would be talking about how great they are." That's not at all what she found.

Right off the bat, Miriam told me, "Everybody really let their guard down and talked about the things that were troubling them. The confusion they felt, changes in their careers, the lack of satisfaction in their lives after having kids and staying home."

The meeting, as is usually the case with these groups, became a blend of peer counseling, confidential sharing, and personal growth. For Miriam, it was eye-opening.

"I realized that most of the things in my life had become obligations rather than choices. All I really did was go to work and take care of my kids, but I wasn't getting joy out of either. I saw I needed to put creativity and art back into my life. That was a very profound and important thing for me to learn."

"You got that from one meeting?" I asked.

"I did. It was amazing."

Whether the groups met regularly or sporadically, they were rich sources of personal enlightenment. Heidi Robertson told me about "a wonderful nurturing group of female executives, typically the highest placed in their organizations. Every year we have an 'appraise your life' evening where we look at things like: What is giving you joy? What is impeding your life? What are you going to do to put more joy in your life? It is the most loving and nurturing experience that I can think of. It's been very helpful."

This last meeting, she said, was totally transforming. "I was working with computers and was absolutely physically and emotionally exhausted. Everybody just split up laughing when I said, 'I don't even like computers.' Then they asked me, seriously, 'What do you like?' The appreciation, understanding, sympathy, and empathy that came out of the group was incredible." She quit her job soon after that evening and decided to become a financial adviser.

PROFESSIONAL SUPPORT

In the workplace, True Believers and Way Showers are otherwise known as mentors and role models. Mentors have long been considered the most valuable asset to a woman's career. "A powerful mentor can turn the glass ceiling into a glass elevator to the executive suite," proclaimed *Investors Business Daily* (April 25, 2000). Conversely, the absence of a mentor has been shown to significantly thwart a woman's chances for advancement, turning a "glass ceiling into a concrete one," according to Catalyst, a nonprofit organization dedicated to advancing women in business.

Every woman I interviewed had a Way Shower who initiated her into the secrets of success. But here again, we often have the misconception that unless such a guide falls in our lap, we're out of luck. Or that an adviser must have advanced to a certain level to be credible. That's simply not true. Many of the women I interviewed deliberately pursued a protégé relationship with someone they respected but didn't necessarily know. And, frequently, those relationships didn't fit the standard picture of what we expect a mentor to look like.

When publicist Jodee Blanco first started her career as an intern at MTV, she was introduced to one of the cofounders. "I remember telling him, 'I have so much respect for you, I'm going to ask for your guidance throughout my career.' He was so flattered that to this day he still gets me out of messes."

From that early experience, Jodee has this advice for women:

"Don't wait for a mentor to be ushered into your life. You can assemble them as if they were your own personal motivational army. You don't necessarily say to someone, 'I want you to be my mentor,' but you can say, 'Would you mind if I bounce some ideas off you? I'd really love your advice.' Most people who are seasoned are flattered and usually respond."

Assembling our own motivational army is a terrific idea and easier than you might think. You can recruit mentors from all sorts of places.

Harriett Simon Salinger hired a coach to help her get back on her feet after her bankruptcy. "It wasn't that she told me what to do, but at least I had a partner. That's what coaching provides. I didn't want to get sidetracked. I have a history of that. She helped me stay on purpose and true to my intentions."

Quite a few of the six-figure women paid someone to give them discipline, direction, validation, and sometimes a different point of view.

"The worst mistake I ever made in my business is that I didn't get an outside coach to come in sooner," said marketing consultant Vickie Sullivan. "I thought it would be too expensive and I had never paid for a consultant before; I always went through the business center at the community college. But they never spent enough time really looking deep into the issues." So she signed up with a "guru in the industry" who zeroed right in on her problem—she was undercharging.

"'You are working way too hard,' he told me. 'You just need to bump up your fees.' He kicked my butt several times. He'd tell me, 'Vickie, you're being silly here. I promise you can get the money, but you have to ask.' We'd role-play. He'd tell me I wasn't coming off strong enough. 'You know your services are good, start acting like they are!' I'd say, 'But people have so many choices,' and he'd say, 'You're the *only one* who does what you do just the way you do it. Tell them that.' He helped me think bigger."

Debra Situ sought coaching after joining a start-up where the intense pressure to perform began taking its toll. "What a good coach does is give you perspective," Debra explained. "I'd get so scared and emotional, but my coach would show me that even if the job ends there will be another one. She motivates me, helps me identify my goals, and brings some balance into my life so I feel more in control."

Just recently, Debra found herself procrastinating on a project. "I just didn't want to do it. So I phoned my coach and she helped me structure my weekend so I saw one friend a day, got my support, cleaned my house, and completed the project."

Coaches come in many guises. I'll never forget when an investment banker described, in a hushed voice, how her mother's lack of self-worth had trickled down to her children. "Every day has been a fight against this idea that I am a failure, unable to accomplish very much, and to say, 'I can do this, I can accomplish this.'" Then she took a deep breath and awkwardly admitted she'd been seeing a therapist. "My female colleagues probably don't have these issues of overcoming internal obstacles in order to achieve success."

I laughed. "You want to bet?" I told her how many women I interviewed were in counseling for that very reason. Is it any wonder? Six-figure women have had to push the boundaries of convention, fight the limitations of their upbringing, go against the gravity of their beliefs, and struggle to gain entry into a world that didn't particularly want them. Without someone to provide psychological insight and emotional support, who knows how many women might have given up too early or never found their way at all. More important than the money, they would have missed knowing the fullness of who they are and the excitement life holds when pursuing a dream.

"I had a wonderful therapist, who helped me change my whole life," business owner Kitty Stuart told me enthusiastically. "I worked really hard with her to overcome a lot of the false ways I was thinking, the little boxes I had myself in. After my divorce, I didn't think I could go out there and make a living of any kind. I didn't even think I could get a job. When I started to create this doll business, she always said, 'Go for it. Get out there and do it.' I feel so fortunate I worked with such an astounding person."

Most successful women had more than one mentor, as was the case with Kitty, whose office assistant also became her mentor. "When I wanted to take another step forward," Kitty recounted, "she'd push me to go out there and do it. But she'd also temper my crazy 'Let's jump in' with 'Have you thought about this or that?' She's a major force in my success."

Kitty even has a mentor she's never met, and probably never will. "My most fabulous mentor is Richard Branson [the British founder of Virgin Air]. Someone advised me once to look for the most successful people I could find and learn from him or her. So that's exactly what I did. I read his book and was so inspired that I built my whole fantastic Barbie business around his concepts and ideas."

Like Kitty, a surprising number of women told me that some of the best advice they ever got came from inspirational books. Others found guidance by watching successful people, men and women. An African American lawyer pointed to a black woman partner in her firm. "Even though I'd never worked with her, just knowing she'd made partner helped me be able to picture myself elevated to that level."

Real estate broker Galina Blackman told me she "learned from the best" by observing the top producer in her company. "She's a fabulous woman. She never gave me any advice per se. I just listened to her, the way she dealt with clients, the way she talked on the phone, the way she presented herself. That helped me tremendously to become a top producer."

Joining a professional network seemed especially important for entrepreneurs, who often worked alone. Catherine Fredman, a freelance writer, recalled the summer she collaborated on a book that had an especially tight deadline. "The coauthor lived in California. We did all our work over the phone. I never left my apartment. It was very lonely. I had no one to talk to except the mailman and the guy who sells newspapers. I told a friend, also an author, I was feeling isolated. So was she. We both burst into tears. We pooled our Rolodexes and started a writers' group. Now there are twenty of us who e-mail frequently and meet for potlucks. I've gotten very good advice from them and made some wonderful friends."

A few years ago, Internet consultant Kitty Reeve cofounded Women in Multimedia 40+, a group of women over forty who work in technology. She attributes the candid conversations at those meetings for her success in becoming a six-figure woman at age fifty-nine.

"Women would share what they were making," she told me. "They'd even stand up and say that when they charged too little, people wouldn't hire them. This was very empowering to me."

Women I interviewed told me over and over how empowering and motivating professional groups are. My favorite story came from Patricia Cloherty, the first president of the Committee of 200, a network of female entrepreneurs. In these meetings, she told me, the women would discuss the ways they grew their company, the challenges they faced, and how they overcame them.

"The whole idea was to encourage women to be risk takers," Pat explained. "That's where the higher rewards come. In the eighties that was a dramatic statement. I'll never forget, I got Georgette Klinger [a cosmetic tycoon] to be a member. She went to the first meeting and when she got back, her own chief financial officer called me and said, 'What do you women do together? Georgette got back from that meeting today and all of a sudden, she wants to grow the business.' I said, 'Tony, that's the whole point.'"

SPIRITUAL SUPPORT

I actually didn't expect this fourth source of support to be mentioned so frequently by six-figure women. But, on further reflection, perhaps I shouldn't have been so surprised. After all, isn't "In God We Trust" emblazoned on every piece of U.S. currency?

"I don't think I could have been so successful if I didn't have faith in a higher being," business owner Claire Prymus told me. "There are times when I get so tired. But with God, I know something bigger is driving me, I can do anything."

Quite a few high-earning women use their faith to give them strength and perspective. They view their jobs as part of a larger plan, a divine calling. They believe that everything that occurs, good or bad, happens for a reason; that their intuition is the ultimate authority; and that their Higher Power is their most profound and trusted ally. Actress Debbie Reynolds, facing bankruptcy and a dwindling career, found both solace and counsel by consulting directly with God and Jesus. "I'll say, 'OK, Boys, why did this happen again? How could You not protect me?' If I talk long enough, I figure out my problem, I get an answer. I feel there is guidance. I wouldn't know how to do it without faith."

Like Debbie, many women depended heavily on their faith for guidance, comfort, courage, and protection.

"I know there's something more out there and this grounds me, it keeps me from getting sucked into the turmoil," said one woman. "I don't know how to say this without sounding mystical," said another, "but I really feel like someone is watching over me, and if I do what's right, everything will work out financially. It's never failed yet."

Entrepreneur Sheila Brooks, who was raised in a ghetto, told me most of the kids she grew up with are dead, in jail, or still impoverished, but she "beat the odds" through hard work and an unshakable faith in a Higher Power. "I truly believe that all things are possible with God. Every day I spend time in meditation and prayer. I thank my Higher Power for everything He has given me. When I do that, I know that no matter how bad things are, I can overcome."

GETTING MORE

No matter how busy these women got, no matter how nerve-racking their day, they made a deliberate effort to carve out time for these True Believers and Way Showers. Whether it was an intimate confidant or an unseen force, they drew on this support, like water from a well, to nourish themselves and blossom in their careers.

As I asked these women how they found their support, I made an intriguing discovery. Each of the strategies we've discussed thus far can be used for increasing your support system as well as your salary. Begin by declaring an intention to attract supportive people into your life and be willing to let go of those who aren't. Then get in the game by joining a group and deliberately networking on a regular basis. Likewise, start speaking up and asking for a hand. Reaching out and soliciting help may be somewhat of a stretch,

10

STRATEGY #7:
OBEY THE RULES OF MONEY

*Rich—The loss of your job makes no difference
to your standard of living.*
—RICHARD RUSSELL, *DOW THEORY LETTERS*

Rich—We work because we want to.
—KATHY, MEMBER OF RPW (RICH PROFESSIONAL WOMEN)

In one of my very first interviews, I asked a woman what it felt like to make six figures. Her response wasn't at all what I expected. "It's astounding to me that I can earn this much and still not feel like I have any money," she declared. Even more astounding was how many other high earners would tell me they felt exactly the same way.

It didn't matter if they were married or single or that they were earning more than 99 percent of the people on this planet. Very few women told me they felt rich. And the sad fact is, *very few are.* Less than half of the six-figure women I spoke to had a net worth over a million dollars, far fewer if you didn't count their home. Fewer still could afford to stop working, even years down the road. Clara, a corporate director, awkwardly admitted, "I know people would laugh and say, 'What! You can't live on $650,000?' but I feel one step away from a refrigerator carton on the street."

especially for the shy and reclusive. But support, like success, is often found just outside our comfort zone.

The surest way to find support, however, is to provide it. Support is a game that everyone wins, the one who gives and the one who receives. Every player is mutually enriched. "When you ask people for help, you're doing them a favor," one woman told me. "And when you do a favor for someone else, it makes you feel better than anything you've done all day." So you want more support? Try giving it. Do a good deed: volunteer for a nonprofit or serve on a charity board; encourage or console someone in need and praise everyone who crosses your path; offer advice to the inexperienced and lend a hand to the seasoned; and when you join the six-figure club, invite another to enlist along with you. "It's one of the most beautiful compensations of life," Ralph Waldo Emerson tells us, "that no one can sincerely try to help another without helping himself." Or said another way: What goes around, comes around.

"How is that possible?" I asked Clara when she told me she didn't have enough to retire.

She answered, "I never thought about my future. I just figured I'd be taken care of. Now that I'm nearing fifty, it's like 'Oh, maybe I should start doing something.'"

It became increasingly apparent, in the course of these conversations, that *making* a lot of money is very different from *having* a lot of money. As such, I noticed six-figure women fell into two distinct categories. The majority were Modest Accumulators—high earners who spent too much and saved too little. Their ample earnings gave them the illusion, but not the security or freedom, of affluence.

The second, and much smaller, group was the Wealth Builders. These women had both substantial salaries and sizable bank balances. They didn't necessarily have the highest incomes, but each had a growing net worth. If they weren't yet millionaires, they were well on their way to becoming ones.

Here's why: They faithfully followed the three-pronged strategy for creating wealth—*spend less, save more, invest wisely*. These three rules of money enabled them to retain and augment their income. A simple strategy, right? But one that has been practiced by too few of our parents, taught in too few of our schools, and therefore was never integrated into many of our lives. Only the Wealth Builders realized, at some point, as did Mary Helen Gillespie, "The biggest challenge is not making the money, but managing the money."

THE TRUTH OF THE MATTER

You may ask why it's even necessary for high earners to worry about managing money if they can easily make a bundle whenever they want. And indeed, many well-heeled women have adopted that very attitude. It's called living from paycheck to paycheck. But just as reliance on a spouse can provide a false sense of security, whopping wages can be just as deceptive and dangerous.

According to *Working Woman* magazine (September 1995), the most expensive mistake a woman makes is assuming her current financial situation is permanent. The truth is:

- In any given period, three out of four women face a major life change, and fewer than half are financially prepared.
- Fifty percent of all marriages end in divorce; 48 percent end with the husband's death (average age of widowhood: fifty-six).
- Seven out of ten women never retire because they can't afford to.
- One in three women owes more in credit card debt than she has in her retirement account.
- Among women between the ages of thirty-five and fifty-five, one-half to two-thirds will be impoverished by age seventy.

High earners are as vulnerable to hard times and sudden change as anyone else. Ignoring the rules of money puts them at an especially high risk. I found it heartbreaking to hear confessions such as this one from Clara, who made $650,000 but never bothered to take care of it: "Money gives you power over your destiny, the power to get out of the rat race, but you obviously have to save and invest the money. If I could, I'd move to Vermont and get off this treadmill. But I can't do that."

Experts tell us that we'll need 70 to 80 percent of our gross income to sustain our lifestyle after retirement. That requires a considerable nest egg. "It was a real eye-opener when I saw I needed several million dollars to retire," said a woman who had just run a financial projection. Most of the women I spoke to had no idea how much they needed or if they were anywhere near those goals. Many suspected they weren't. Women repeatedly told me: "I know I should do more with my money, but . . . " Only their excuses varied:

- From an executive: "Letting my husband worry about the money made me feel more womanly."
- From an entrepreneur: "I became so driven by my work, I lost sight of my finances."
- From a consultant: "Finance just doesn't interest me. It's boring."
- From a writer: "I was the creative one. Money wasn't important. Oh, how wrong I was."
- From a senior vice president: "I truly believed someone else would take care of it all while I was busy making it."

But underneath their wide-ranging excuses lurked the real reason for their passivity—in a word, fear. Shortly after our interview, I received an e-mail from makeup artist Kris Evans. "I realized I didn't take care of money because I didn't want to know what I had or didn't have," she wrote. "Growing up, we just scraped by, so I was always afraid of not having enough. Denial meant safety to me. Out of sight meant out of mind."

Like Kris, too many women have been masking their fear with make-believe. But such complacency has put them on what one study calls "a collision course with reality." Let me show you what this collision course could look like.

I was once a guest on a television talk show. The subject: millionaires who went broke. Among the guests were an ambitious entrepreneur, a famous singer, and a big-shot lawyer. These were bright, successful people who once earned millions but were now living on food stamps, out on the street, or hounded by creditors. Obviously, this was a show designed for heavy melodrama and high ratings. But wedged in between the tales of trauma was a critical message: *It's not what we have but what we* do *with what we have that gives us or denies us financial security.*

The guests pointed to a conniving business partner, a crushing divorce, or a cruel blow of fate as the source of their insolvency. But, in truth, the real culprit was their own inertia. Each of them had continued abusing, mismanaging, or neglecting their finances until they were virtually penniless.

FOLLOW THE RULES

If this could happen to them, it could easily happen to any one of us. But it doesn't have to. From these interviews and from my own experience, I've learned that economic independence is a whole lot simpler than you think. (Though there is a whole industry hell-bent on convincing you otherwise.) You don't need a lot of time to get smart. Nor do you need a lot of money to create wealth. In fact, you could actually accumulate millions regardless of your current income. While the best time to start is when you're young, you're never too old to begin. The biggest risk you take, at any age, is to do nothing at all.

What wealth building does require is consistent application of the three rules of money. You simply must make the following actions a way of life. You must do all three. There are no exceptions.

1. Spend less than you earn.

2. Pay yourself first.

3. Put your money to work.

SPEND LESS

Wealth doesn't come from what you make, but from what you don't spend. For the most part, the women I interviewed lived within their means. That didn't mean they were miserly. Except for a handful of tightwads, most of them spent lavishly, especially on clothes, home furnishings, travel, entertainment, and convenience. Their consumer patterns, however, had a double personality. They could easily drop hundreds of dollars on a pair of shoes and at the same time "become apoplectic about paying for a parking space." They wouldn't think twice about hiring someone to walk their dogs or deliver their meals but "refuse to buy sea bass because it's twice as expensive as salmon."

This dueling blend of extravagance and thrift served as a built-in system of checks and balances, a self-imposed safeguard against overindulgence. Consequently, very, very few six-figure women had credit card debt. Overall, I'd classify high earners as *conscious spenders.*

"I wouldn't call myself tight or frugal, but I don't spend giant wads of money, either," said marketing consultant Marci Blaze. "I am conscious. Very conscious. I know what we can afford. And I spend in direct proportion to my ability to replace it."

Most six-figure women were like Marci. They never spent more than they earned, though their considerable incomes gave them plenty of leeway. Some of them knew, down to the penny, not only how much they were spending but exactly where they were spending it. And they could quickly adapt to fluctuating circumstances. "I learned to have a self-regulating mechanism in my brain that said, I only have this much money, so I can't spend any more," said an entrepreneur. When business was slow, she told me, "It just meant I didn't go shopping as much."

Sometimes, however, this "self-regulating mechanism" was slow to kick in. It wasn't unusual for many high earners to go overboard, particularly at the beginning of their careers after a lifetime of poverty or years of low-paying jobs. Many women told me that as their earnings went up, so did their expenditures.

"I was like a kid in a candy store," said Karen Page, referring to life after business school. "I was so tired of having a negative income for two years. When I suddenly started making money, I bought expensive shoes, suits, accessories. It was the first time I was able to indulge myself. I hadn't grown up like that. But I learned to adjust and don't spend like that anymore."

"As my income increased," former journalist Mary Helen Gillespie admitted, "I went on a binge. But after a while, you run out of things to buy. I mean, how many living room rugs can you use? Now I'm more conscious about shopping. I still shop at Saks, but I also go to Target."

"I made an agreement with myself," said Valerie Gerard, now a senior executive. "I could buy whatever I wanted until I hit thirty. Then I would get disciplined. So I got all these good clothes and nice things for my apartment. Then the day I hit thirty, I stopped."

These women, all Wealth Builders, were spenders who kept the brakes on, controlling their binges so they didn't incur debt. There were others, though only a few, who used money like Novocain to numb the pain in their lives or the pressures at work. And they all got into trouble. They justified their shopping sprees with thoughts like "I'm going through a divorce. I deserve this" or "I hate my job. At least I can enjoy my life." Their denial produced considerable debt, more than $20,000 on average. And it wasn't because these women were high rollers; they just weren't honest with themselves. As Harriett Simon Salinger told me about her bankruptcy, "I wasn't a big spender, but I'd spend more than was coming in. I was in total denial."

Getting out of denial is a prerequisite for prosperity. I vividly remember my interview with a highly paid and very frazzled physician who once thought she "only" owed a few hundred dollars. But when she added up the balance on each of her many credit cards, the total was in the thousands. Years later, she's still paying it off. "I despise this debt hanging over my head," she told me with a loaded sigh.

Credit card debt is insidious but not insurmountable. No matter how much you make, it will so erode earnings as to make wealth virtually impossible. The average American has a debt balance of $5,391. Making minimum payments, that will take thirty-two years to pay off because 75 percent of what you pay goes toward the accumulating interest. However, many of the Wealth Builders I interviewed had risen from the ashes of their once reckless spending.

A financial planner who grew up poor but was now worth more than $5 million told me, "Years ago I was spending like crazy and couldn't pay off my credit cards. Then one day I said, 'OK, it's time to take the same advice you give your clients. You have to pay off your credit card debt.' Once I was free of that, I couldn't believe how great it felt. I hated having debt so much I've never spent like that again."

The women who worked their way out of debt usually did so by taking a series of steps. (I always ask underearners in my groups to do these same steps whether or not they have debt. The experience is not only enlightening but also often transforming.)

- They sought help (from a book, a counselor, or a support
  group like Debtors Anonymous).

- They stopped using credit cards.
- They lowered their interest payments (by negotiating with creditors or transferring the balance to a lower-interest card).
- They got clarity (by writing down everything they spent).
- They stopped overspending (by putting their expenses into categories, they saw where to make cuts).
- They paid down their debt as quickly as they could.

In her early twenties, Stephanie Astic was living on credit cards, unable to make payments and sinking deeper into debt, until she went to a workshop on women and money. The instructor, she recalled, "told us to freeze our credit cards. Literally! That's what I did. I went home, put all my cards in a bowl of water, stuck them in the freezer, and left them there."

The instructor also asked if anyone even knew what interest rates they were paying on their cards. "I had no idea I was paying twenty percent," said Stephanie, who immediately consolidated her payments onto one card that charged lower interest.

"There was a lot of stuff I didn't know. I had to come out of that denial and look at what I was making, how much debt I was in, and how I was going to make it work."

She broke through her denial by scrutinizing her spending. "I recorded everything I spent. Every dime. Every penny. When I tracked my spending, I saw where the money was going. I was spending way too much on clothes and cabs. So I put myself on a budget, which I was in huge resistance to at first."

As Stephanie overcame her resistance and started making changes, she felt more in control in her whole life.

"It took some time, but as I got bigger jobs, I'd immediately put aside more money to bring down my debt. I knew that when I got debt free, my life would be different. And that's what happened."

Two years ago, at age twenty-nine, when she was finally solvent, Stephanie's career began to flourish.

"It happened right at the same time. There definitely is a relationship. Not having debt gave me the freedom to go out there and make more money. I didn't feel so constricted by my limitations. I felt empowered."

These days Stephanie warns the young women she meets, "Watch out for credit cards. They're dangerous." Most of the women I was speaking to, unlike Stephanie, hardly ever abused their credit, were conscious spenders, and rarely incurred debt. So the question is: Why weren't more of these six-figure women wealthy? The answer is: Spending less is only the first part of a three-part strategy. It's an important part, to be sure, but incomplete without the others.

SAVE MORE

Savings is where six-figure women veer off the wealth-building track. This really hit home when I interviewed two women back to back. Both were in their forties. Both earned about $120,000 a year. Both described themselves as frugal. But one was worth millions, the other a mere fraction of that.

"I don't save as much as I should," one of them told me. "I have no debt. I have some emergency savings. But most of my income goes into our house and vacations."

"I save everything," said the other. "I automatically have one-third of my check put into savings, one-third is deducted for the government, and I live on the rest."

It's obvious which woman was rich: the one who combined *conscious spending with consistent savings*, a recipe for wealth that's almost as old as money itself.

In 1926, George S. Clason, publisher of the first road atlas of the United States, wrote a slim volume of parables about Babylonia, once the wealthiest city in the world. *The Richest Man in Babylon* has become a modern classic that some people, including me, consider among the best finance books ever written. When we first meet the richest man in Babylon, he is telling friends the secret to his fortune.

"I found the road to wealth," he tells them, "when I decided that *a part of all I earn is mine to keep.*" (Italics are mine.) The men look at him incredulously. "Is that all?" one asks, insisting that *of course* everything he makes is his to keep. The wealthy man just shakes his head. "You fool, you pay everyone but yourself," he cries, pointing to the clothing sellers, sandal makers, and wine merchants. Instead, the rich man counsels them, pay yourself first. *"For every 10 coins thou places in thy purse, take out for use but nine."* (Italics are mine.)

PAY YOURSELF FIRST

This is the way that Wealth Builders live—*a part of all they earn goes into their personal savings on a regular basis.* I've watched many underearners transform small salaries into hefty bank balances by becoming prodigious savers. Recently, one of them proudly announced to the group, "I used to spend my money, and whatever I had left, I'd pay what bills I could. Now, every month, I write a check to myself first, then I pay my bills, and whatever is left, I can spend. It's amazing how fast it adds up." And another, an artist with an irregular income, reported back to us: "Whenever I sell a painting, I immediately take part of what I make and put it in savings. I use the rest for bills. It feels great."

Discipline, not deprivation, is the ticket to financial security.

"I don't deny myself anything I want," said a middle-aged woman who had become quite wealthy in the decade since her divorce. "But I am also a big saver. I save part of every dollar I make. It is like I never got it. It isn't even a conversation. It just goes into savings automatically."

"I've not lived frugally, but smartly," said another woman who became wealthy in her thirties. "I imposed a discipline on myself a long time ago. Every time I got a raise I would just have it automatically deducted into savings. I live on a steady income stream that hasn't gone up for years because I'm socking it away."

Likewise, another wealthy thirty-year-old said, "I'm a great saver. That doesn't mean I don't spend money on myself. If I see a great pair of shoes, I'll buy them. But since my first paycheck, I've put money in the bank. My first check was two hundred dollars working retail, and I put twenty-five dollars in the bank. I always put a decent percentage away. The bank does it automatically."

Discipline is easy if done automatically. All it takes is a call to the bank; they'll send you a form to fill out. It's that simple. You won't miss what you don't see. And the money will add up surprisingly fast. But keep this thought in mind: The money you're putting away is for an unforeseen emergency, not an unexpected shoe sale. Savings should be, as one high earner described it, "sacrosanct, something I never touch, so if anything happens, I know I have it."

Stephanie French was grateful she continued to tuck money away, even after she married a wealthy man, because last year the marriage abruptly ended. "We were living in an apartment worth over a million dollars," she told me. "I didn't want to move my kids in the middle of the divorce so I bought the apartment. I could do that because I've saved over all this time."

Similarly, Heidi Robertson, who had saved a fortune by the time she was in her forties, discovered, "that million dollars in the bank gave me freedom." Freedom to quit her job, do some charity work, spend time with her family, go on a cruise with her husband, and, a year later, take a dream job with a huge cut in pay.

"It'll take me two years to get back to six figures," she told me. "The decreased paycheck is immaterial, because I have a lot of savings and am financially secure. If I were struggling to pay my bills this would be a whole different conversation."

Cash in the bank is a buffer against debt or undue sacrifice, a prudent reserve for unpredictable events and the pursuit of dreams. But you can be sure that Heidi's financial freedom didn't come from keeping her entire savings in cash. Just as wealth won't happen if you're paying 20 percent interest to Visa, it's also unattainable if all your money is earning 2 or 3 percent in the bank.

INVEST WISELY

Seven years ago, Mary Helen Gillespie, a former journalist, wrote a series of articles about retirement for women. "That was my personal wake-up call," she told me. "We live longer and make less. What really scares me is inflation. I want to be able to have a quality life when I'm older, so I realized I need to invest to stay ahead of inflation."

Mary Helen was right to be concerned. Even the wealthiest Americans, those with earnings over $200,000 or net worths over $3 million, told a *USA Today* survey (May 21, 1996) that their biggest worry was "that inflation will erode their retirement income, forcing them to reduce their standard of living."

Inflation is a ravenous creature that devours our dollars like a caterpillar on a leaf—slowly, methodically, little bits at a time. If inflation averages 3 percent a year, and we have our money in a 3 percent savings account, the buying power of that cash will be halved in twenty years. If inflation rises to 4 percent, it'll only take fifteen years. That means that $50 pair of jeans will cost you more than $100 in less than a decade. And that $100,000 you sock away today will shrink to $45,000 in even less time.

The only way to counter the ravages of rising prices is to make sure at least some of your savings is working harder than it would in a bank. Economic independence is made possible by the third rule of money—invest wisely. Or, in the words of the wealthy Babylonian: "Learn to make your gold work for you. Make it your slave, make its children and its children's children work for you." He was describing the power of compounding: putting money in assets that will grow over time, with earnings building on earnings. Surprisingly, and unfortunately, many of the women I interviewed were either investing too conservatively or not investing altogether, making them unwary victims of the rising cost of living.

Why would so many otherwise intelligent women ignore their finances? In large part, they're overloaded. As one woman explained, "Most of us are incredibly busy. We work long hours. Even though you realize it's the most important thing you can do with your money, investing gets crowded out." Important as it is, there's so much information and so many options that, as one survey confirmed, financial decisions seem so "forbidding and complicated" that many conclude "Why bother?"

The truth is, managing money is not all that complex (see Investing Basics, page 266). The standard rule of thumb is this:

- Money you need in the next five to seven years—for emergencies, unexpected expenses, or short-term goals—should be in cash or cash equivalents like money market funds, CDs, or short-term treasuries.

- Money you will need in the next seven to ten years should be in a mix of stocks, bonds, and cash.
- Money you won't need for ten or more years should be mostly in stocks.

When Eileen Michaels first left nursing to become a stockbroker, she asked her colleagues how she should invest $500, which was all she had at the time. Everyone told her $500 wasn't enough to put in the market, except for one man. "That's ridiculous," he told her. "It is the other way around. It is not how much money you have that matters. It is the percentage of return you get. You won't ever have money until you start putting money to work. In the money conversation, people go, 'Oh, when I have the money then I'll invest.' That doesn't work."

This wise man's advice would eventually make Eileen wealthy. It can do the same for you. "This is the process by which wealth is accumulated," the wealthy Babylonian says. "First in small sums then in larger ones as we learn and grow more capable."

I recently read in our local newspaper about a librarian who made $8,500 a year and left a $2.2 million estate, and elsewhere, about a ninety-four-year-old bookkeeper who earned even less and was worth over $8 million at her death. According to the articles, both these women derived their wealth from carefully investing their earnings. It doesn't take a huge salary or a stingy lifestyle to end up with a sizable net worth. Given time to compound, small amounts consistently invested can reap enormous rewards.

A twenty-year-old has to invest only $1,025 a year in a fund growing 11 percent annually (the average rate of return for stocks) to make $1 million by age sixty-five. A thirty-five-year-old needs to put $5,000 a year in that same fund to have $1 million by age sixty-five. A fifty-year-old needs $29,000 a year, and a fifty-five-year-old $60,000 a year.

If only we all had started investing in our twenties! The fact is, most wealthy women I interviewed didn't begin until they were much older. And then discipline was key, especially for busy people in consuming jobs who might otherwise procrastinate, act impulsively, or simply forget. Anyone can become a disciplined investor by taking four simple steps.

1. Automate.

Just as Wealth Builders automatically transfer money from their paycheck to their savings account, they do the same with investing. They make arrangements for a specific sum to be deducted from their bank account or paychecks and deposited in their brokerage accounts. They max out their tax-deferred retirement accounts first, and then regularly put money into mutual funds or individual equities.

For example, one entrepreneur told me, "Every year, I put thirty thousand dollars into a SEP-IRA. Every month, I have three thousand dollars transferred into a money market account, three thousand dollars into an annuity, and five hundred dollars each into different mutual funds." Another did the same with an education fund for her son. "Each week a certain amount of money is taken out of my paycheck for his education and stuck in a credit union somewhere I don't even see."

Automatic investing is important, because when left to their own devices, I'd hear something very different—even if they worked in the field! I remember a banker telling me regretfully, "I'm terrible at investing. I do it haphazardly.

Money will come in and sit for a long time, uninvested, in cash, not earning what it should. There's a part of me that says I should be doing this myself, and another part that says I don't even know where to start." Start with a call to your bank to arrange regular transfers.

2. Delegate.

Practically every Wealth Builder I spoke to worked with financial professionals, or they were considering doing so, even if they were employed in the financial field themselves. Beth Sawi, for example, CAO of Charles Schwab, hired someone to manage her money. "Not because I couldn't do it," she explained. "But because I'm busy making a six-figure income. I look at what I pay my adviser. I could save so much money. But when I get a bonus check, it would sit in my checking account. I'd forget to make tax-free gifts to my kids. I wouldn't do anything without this guy helping me."

These women all sought professional help for the same reason: to get them on track and keep them on track. "I was giving it no time," said a woman who has been buying stocks for herself since she was a teen. "I wasn't doing the research I should. I had learned enough to know that just because a company has a good product, it's not enough of a reason to buy their stock. I finally got a financial adviser."

Just as important as picking equities was how financial advisers helped these women open their eyes.

"Until a couple of years ago," one woman told me, "I didn't realize that all my money was going back into my business. My accountant showed me I wasn't investing wisely." The accountant referred her to a financial planner. Her husband went with her.

"The first thing the planner did was outline our financial position, which was very revealing. He asked questions about where we wanted to go individually and together like: When do you want to retire? How much will you need to live on when you retire? What are your expenses? And how much will you need to save to do that? He made us look more carefully at how we were investing, how our portfolio was balanced, how we were going to get to that retirement number."

3. *Educate.*

Delegating didn't mean Wealth Builders handed over their money and went to sleep. Rather, as one woman said, "My husband takes care of our investments. But since it's my money, we discuss it all the time. I subscribe to the *Economist*, attend lectures on finance, and always read the finance section of the *Tribune* every day so I understand what's going on."

Wealth-building women make it a point to participate in financial decisions from a place of knowledge, *not* fear, ignorance, or habit. Although they are extremely busy, they find ways to stay informed.

Lori, who ran a construction business, described herself as "an information hog. I use the info to be more confident in the decisions I make. I don't have time, but how can I do well or plan for my kids' future if I don't do these things? I integrate them into my life. I read *Fortune, Money,* the *Wall Street Journal* at night or over coffee."

Stephanie Astic, a new investor, admits her broker "makes a lot of the decisions, but I am starting to learn more. I go on-line and I read during my downtime. I actually enjoy it. I got a subscription to *Crain's*, a weekly business magazine. I made a commitment to read, to see what's out there, what's happening, who's merging. I didn't used to think it had any impact on me. Now I feel it is important. I want to know."

4. Communicate.

"I've picked up a lot along the way from other people I know who invest," one woman told me, and so have I. My interviews with savvy women for my last book showed me how much you can learn by talking to smart people. The interviews for this book only confirmed it. To this day, every time I meet anyone who knows anything about finances, I'll pick his or her brain, asking questions like: How do you manage your money? What have you learned? What advice can you give me?

But, as you already know, talking about money is not always easy. For some of us it's embarrassing. We feel too dumb, too poor, too rich, too something. For many, money is still a taboo topic. "Nice girls don't talk about money," our mothers warned us.

That warning is rubbish and should be discarded immediately. Our silence around money is what keeps us stuck. And it's not just practical information we should be seeking. We also need to talk about our personal issues around money. It's deeply comforting and extremely instructive to share individual struggles and to vent fears and frustrations.

"To hear the difficulties others have had is very affirming," exclaimed a woman about her experience in an investment club. "I always struggled to figure this stuff out. Now I feel a lot better knowing I'm not the only one."

Many of the women I interviewed were members of investment clubs for precisely that reason—to commiserate with others as well as educate themselves. Karen Page had just helped start a club with other Harvard alumnae when I interviewed her. "It's amazing to all of us, some who are very, very successful, how little we all knew about investing and how much we're helping each other learn. It's been very eye-opening to realize you're not alone. You'd be surprised at the number of women in this group who until we started kept things tucked away in a savings account earning three percent. We're helping each other."

PUTTING IT ALL TOGETHER.

Anyone at any time can make the transition from Modest Accumulator to Wealth Builder. As Kris Evans reported in her recent e-mail, she's well into the process of making the shift. "I had to have the courage to face what I was dreading no matter what."

After years of avoidance, she finally took a hard look at her financial situation. And she didn't like what she saw.

"My husband and I had a stock portfolio for years, but we'd never shown much interest in it. When I started looking at the account I saw it wasn't much. I thought we had a lot more. It hadn't been mismanaged, just neglected."

Instead of going back into denial, she went into action. "I started reading the *Wall Street Journal, Smart Money,* and the local newspaper. I bought a number of books you recommended. I listened to what was happening in the world because it really affects our markets. I joined an investment club filled with wonderful friends who are so supportive. I reevaluated all my investments and actually understood what I was doing. I started putting more money away every month. I contacted a broker who handles some of the people in my investment club. The fear I had just making that phone call was overwhelming because I didn't think I knew enough to speak to this guy. But I actually carried on a coherent conversation and understood everything he advised me to do."

I could almost feel her pride filling my computer screen. "For the first time in my adult life," she wrote, "I'm taking responsibility for my money. I'm now not only a successful businesswoman but an up-and-coming investment maven."

BECOMING AN INVESTMENT MAVEN

On page 266 are the basics you need to know to become an investment maven, a quick lesson in Wealth Building 101. If you want more information, which hopefully you do, you'll find all kinds of resources listed in the appendix.

One final word: Make sure you have money in your own name. Even if you're supremely happy with your partner, it's important to have your own financial identity. The women I interviewed may have had joint accounts for shared expenses, but almost without exception, they each had bank accounts, credit cards, and investment portfolios in their own name. In part, it's a matter of self-protection. I've heard too many horror stories from women who couldn't get credit or had all kinds of legal problems after losing a husband through death or divorce because everything was listed under their spouse's name.

But there's also a psychological component. A separate financial identity makes a major personal statement. I found it fascinating how many women in my groups, on their own, with no coaching from me, came to this same conclusion. Gradually, they began extricating themselves from the communal pot, opening individual accounts, even while maintaining the shared ones. It had nothing to do with their relationships. It had everything to do with their self-concept. Putting money in your name is about growing up, becoming an adult, claiming your sovereignty over your own life.

Which brings us to the next, and final, chapter. There's still one more secret we haven't discussed, one more fundamental attribute that, as I see it, will be the deciding factor in your future success.

CLAIMING OUR POWER

The only question that matters is "Am I living in a way
that is deeply satisfying and truly expresses me?"
—CARL ROGERS

Our deepest fear is not that we are inadequate.
Our deepest fear is that we are powerful beyond measure.
It is our light, not our darkness, that frightens us.
—NELSON MANDELA

In the beginning, I thought I was writing a book about money. Well, I wasn't, not really. Money is merely the metaphor. I'm convinced that although there are many reasons why women have difficulty making and/or managing money, more often than not it all comes down to one common denominator—our fear of power.

What scares us most about financial success is not that we may fall short but that we may actually take flight and discover that we are, indeed, "powerful beyond measure." For many of us, that's the very thing we're trying to avoid.

When we claim our power, we raise the stakes. Power insists that we become responsible adults, the primary authority in our lives, autonomous, accountable, and as singer/songwriter Helen Reddy crooned, "too big to ignore." That's precisely what's so scary!

"This fear of power is perfectly understandable," explained psychotherapist Olivia Mellan, coauthor of *Money Shy to Money Sure.* It's embedded in our collective unconscious. "Powerful women," she explained, "were burned at the stake."

Although more women are beginning to step into their power, for many, it's still a new thing, Olivia told me. "We aren't quite sure how to handle it. And a lot of us are afraid."

A woman afraid of her power is like an eagle afraid of its wings. We were born to use power. It's who we are, why we're here, how we make our way in the world. I am reminded of a story of a Zen monk who, when asked the secret of Buddha's smile, replied, "It can only be that he smiles at himself for searching all those years for what he already possesses." We, too, may smile at ourselves when we finally figure it out. As I now see it, that's what this book is really about: *reclaiming our power that lies dormant within by realizing our potential, expressing our passion, and, for that, being paid properly.*

Financial independence epitomizes power. Interestingly, the word *money* derives from the Latin feminine noun *moneta.* Moneta was the name for Juno, queen mother of heaven, in whose temple money was minted. Making money is part of our heritage, a legacy it's time we embrace.

30 × 10 = 300

WHAT IS POWER?

In the 1960s, Betty Friedan identified "a problem with no name," which was women's confinement to home and their exclusion from creative expression. As soon as her book *The Feminine Mystique* hit the shelves, a tidal wave of women flooded the job market in search of creative outlets and tangible reward. Today, forty years later, we've flexed our creative muscles, tested our mettle, and proved we could make it. Now we've come to the next phase of our evolution, the next logical step in women's liberation. And we're up against a new hurdle. Call it the "problem that keeps us powerless." We're not paid what we're worth. By restricting our earning potential we're repressing our personal power.

Believe me, there's no better way to limit your feeling of power than by curbing the flow of your funds. Less money not only reduces your options but also creates diversions. If you're preoccupied with paying off debt, you don't have time to deal with the central and more provocative questions: How can I become more of who I really am? How can I live more fully?

Part of the problem stems from our misunderstanding of what power really is. Power, by definition, is the ability to make something happen. From a masculine perspective, that usually means authority, control, and dominance. But according to a cover story in *Fortune* magazine (October 16, 2000), "Women feel powerful when they are making a difference and expanding their own capabilities." And this was my observation as well. To a woman, power means independence, influence, and impact, or as a friend put it, "to effect what I want in my life." This is the power we're seeking, *real power*, the ability to choose how we live, to be in control of our journey. *A powerful woman is one who knows who she is and chooses to express that in the world.*

A prime example is Beth Sawi, CAO of Charles Schwab brokerage firm. Several years ago, after seventeen years at Schwab and in line to be CEO, Beth left the company to write a book. She had no guarantee she could get her job back after the book was finished or if things didn't work out.

"There was a certain amount of turmoil," she told me. "But I'd always wanted to be a writer, and now I had something to write about."

She gave herself four months to mull it over. "Was this really what I wanted, to write a book? Yes. Was it my ambition to be a CEO? A tiny bit. But you have to make choices."

Beth made her choice. She took her husband and two kids to Italy for a year, rented an apartment, wrote a wonderful book, *Coming Up for Air: How to Build a Balanced Life in a Workaholic World*, and had a marvelous experience. When she returned, Schwab welcomed her back. If they hadn't, she was confident she'd find another job. "Writing a book showed me a talent I never knew I had. It was great to say I can turn my back on corporate America. Everyone was envious when they heard what I did."

A woman like Beth, who uses her money to pursue a dream, live out her values, and make an impact on others, is undeniably a powerful person. Another six-figure woman explained it this way: "Power is an internal sense of knowing yourself, and that doesn't require money. But having money allows you to express your power in different ways. I can take a month off and go to Nepal or write a check to someone in trouble, and have the joy of doing it, knowing I made a difference."

Sounds wonderful, right? Then why is claiming our power so scary?

THE COLLECTIVE BRAINWASH

Simply put: We fear what we don't understand. Women don't understand power, and it's obvious why. Money, like sex, is a powerful force. The only way to control access to such powerful forces is with equally powerful taboos. The world's gone to great lengths to keep us in the dark. Until a century ago, a woman could not attend college, enter a profession, keep her earnings, own property, obtain credit, or cast a vote. We were the property of our fathers or husbands.

"Women had fewer rights than a lunatic—a male one—in an insane asylum," a syndicated columnist quipped. Still today, there are no positive words for a powerful woman (think: bitch or ball-breaker) just as there are none for a sexual one (think: nymphomaniac or whore).

In his 1970s groundbreaking study of adult development, Daniel Levinson found that "The Dream," which he defined as "an imagined possibility that generates excitement and vitality" played a "powerful and persuasive role" in a healthy maturing process. "Those who betray their dream," he warned us, "will later deal with the consequences." Those of us who, in supporting someone else's dream, betrayed our own understand the consequences all too well.

As Marie Wilson, the former director of the Ms Foundation, explained, "Between the ages of nine and fifteen, girls lose who they really are, who they want to be, and become what society wants."

My twenty-something daughters tell me this doesn't hold true as much for their generation, but many of us over thirty-five will easily relate. We were groomed to collaborate, not compete; to bolster others rather than achieve our own goals; to marry a doctor instead of becoming one. This "inhibition of a girl's natural aggression begins early," asserts psychiatrist David W. Krueger, the author of *Emotional Business*. "The emphasis is on getting along, not competition, on helping others rather than achieving personal goals."

By way of example, he cites a study of popular children's books. The majority of female characters, according to the study, gained their significance from their relationships with men—the wife of a king, the helper of a worker, the admirer of an adventurer. No wonder so many women I spoke to told me, "I gave up a part of myself so my family would approve." For most of my life, I felt the same way.

The message that's been hammered into our heads, both implicitly and explicitly, is: Our needs don't count, others come first. We were carefully groomed to be victims, acquiring our clout through compliance or charm. Eighteenth-century philosopher Jean-Jacques Rousseau couldn't have made it any clearer: "A woman's dignity consists of being unknown to the world; her glory is in the esteem of her husband, her pleasure in the happiness of her family." Shakespeare, as usual, was pithier: "Frailty, thy name is woman."

So we became the "second sex," living in reflected light, the nurturers and caretakers. There is nothing wrong with nurturing or caring for others, as long as we aren't slicing off chunks of our soul to conform to an image that is not of our choosing, stunting our own growth for the benefit of others.

Practically every woman I interviewed considered her family and friends, especially her children, her utmost priority. But she entered those relationships by design, a reciprocal meeting of needs. In the end, obligatory or guilt-driven self-denial is always undermining, leading to anger, resentment, and pain. An empty vessel has little to offer. Moreover, giving to others without first taking care of ourselves financially and otherwise is inevitably an act of self-sabotage.

A brand-new high earner became very emotional, to the point of tears, as she revealed a pattern she was struggling to break. "Every time I started to get ahead financially, I'd make a big financial commitment to my kids," she told me.

She had recently given her daughter $1,000 for school and then rented a big house so her son could move in, neither of which she could afford. "I had no business doing those things. I love helping my kids, but I put their needs before mine."

When her son asked for a loan to make a down payment on a condo, she finally put her foot down. "I got tired of making money and having nothing to show for it. The shift came from the pain of ending up with all the pain," she explained. "I'd never said no before because I was too embarrassed."

But she recognized how right it was to do when she overheard her son proudly tell a friend how he was saving to buy a condo. "I realized he wouldn't have had that experience if I had lent him the money. I know it's enabling when you bail people out." Just as it's disabling when you deny your own needs.

RELEASE YOUR POWERFUL SELF

Putting yourself first isn't easy to do, which, I believe, is the primary reason women have difficulty embracing their power. *Recapturing one's power is a self-centered process.* Telling a woman to pay more attention to her needs, to become—dare I say it?—selfish, is like suggesting she shoplift or go without bathing. She'd look at you aghast and immediately protest, "I'm not that kind of woman!" Yet self-focus—putting your needs at the top of the list—is precisely what's required to become a Successful High Earner. The way I see it, claiming our power is an act of self-love.

Attorney Rikki Klieman's story really brought this point home for me. After years of paying off student loans, working in public service where the pay was lousy but the experience invaluable, Rikki went into private practice and "the money began rolling in." As a symbol of her success, she bought a mink coat. "For me, the purchase of that coat was my realization that I had achieved financial independence," Rikki said.

Soon afterward, when she was boarding an airplane, the flight attendant remarked to her, "What a beautiful coat. Someone must really love you." To which Rikki responded, "Yes, I bought it for myself."

This is how you claim your power: by honoring yourself, valuing yourself, taking all your desires to heart. Another six-figure woman, a former underearner who had overcome a lifelong bout with worka-holism, expressed her coming into power this way: "I realized I needed to put myself in the center of my own life, take my needs seriously. It's been a wonderful experience, a personal journey of empowerment, but I had no idea it would be so difficult."

It's always difficult to deviate from the norm, especially a long-prescribed role, like trying to write with your nondominant hand. It feels awkward, unnatural, as if you're doing something wrong. Your immediate impulse is to go back to your old ways. Whenever we get too close to our personal authority, we're apt to have a similar reac-tion. Our feminine psyche will start emitting signals that are usually misinterpreted as intuition—inexplicable waves of trepidation, ever so slight ripples of fear—compelling us to, as one woman described it, "water myself down."

"We were never trained to be powerful, and it is very uncomfort-able for us," financial adviser Eileen Michaels agreed. "You're called to show up, to be all you can be. Most women don't like it."

"Do you?" I asked.

"Now I do. I didn't in the beginning. I grew up with the notion some man should be taking care of me."

Eileen told me her story: As a young divorcée, trying to find work to support her children, she began having back pains and went to a physical therapist. When the therapist asked, "What's wrong?" Eileen replied, "I feel like my wings are stuck."

"That's how I felt," she said. "It takes a lot of courage to really take a full wingspan."

It requires tremendous fortitude to shake off the myths and mes-sages from the past, to release the imprisoned feminine that is your powerful self, to make your welfare as important as everyone else's. (Not to the exclusion of others', mind you, but *equally important*.) As the psychologist Rollo May reminds us, "Self-love is not only necessary and good, it is a prerequisite for loving others." Self-centered doesn't mean narcissistic—quite the opposite. Women have such an innate desire for interconnectedness that the more authentic their goals, the more their relationships mattered. That's exactly what I found in my interviews. The clearer each woman was about her own needs, the more other people factored into her equation.

When Charlotte Maure started a consulting firm with her husband, she told me, "We spent a whole day asking ourselves: What is important to us? Are we just here to make money? What are our goals, financial and personal? We both agreed we wanted to make a contribution to the firms we worked with. We wanted everybody at the place where we intervened to have an opportunity to be heard, seen, and listened to."

In the same vein, Deb Maloy, a financial planner, told me the reason she chose her field was not only because she loved the work but because "I truly find happiness and joy in helping others. I'm giving people financial confidence, preventing them from making stupid mistakes, and I'm getting paid handsomely for it. It's the best of both worlds."

Restaurant owner Judith Wicks agreed. "I see my business is all about relationships. It's a way of serving others. That's how I find happiness. I've found ways to be of service I'd never dreamed of."

THE HIGH PRICE OF DEPENDENCY

There's another punch line to the mink-coat story. After Rikki's response "I bought it for myself," the stewardess replied, "You know, in the end it's cheaper that way."

Just as claiming our power is an act of self-love, forsaking it is an act of self-betrayal. We pay dearly for deference and dependency. It costs us our autonomy, self-esteem, and peace of mind. As Rikki told me, "I always know that the only person who will never leave me is me. I absolutely adore my husband, but what if he dies? I have this notion if I can't take care of me, no one else will."

Many six-figure women have wrestled with this delicate issue. "I had big dreams that my husband would take care of me financially," said one woman whose husband never became as successful as she had hoped. "But I've learned that I have to be the one responsible for my money. It has been painful to come to that. But with that pain came pride, because I now feel I don't have to depend on anyone. This money buys me freedom. I don't *need* my husband. I could do just fine financially. But I *want* to be with him because I love him."

ROCKING THE BOAT

Be warned: Going against the grain is bound to have repercussions. Change is preceded by choice but often followed by chaos. Claiming your power means rocking the boat, and there will be people in your life who won't want their boat rocked and will be angry at you for doing it. The reason women forfeit their power in the first place is to fit in, be liked, approved of, and accepted. Many of us have spent a lifetime saying yes when we mean no, being nice when mistreated, pretending "it's no big deal" when it is—anything to avoid hurting people's feelings or, worse, making them angry.

"You can't be powerful if you're not willing to be in conflict," says psychologist Linda L. Moore, the author of *Release from Powerlessness*. (Women give away power to avoid discord, she added, but men also give away their power to avoid feeling.)

Our worry is that conflict will disrupt the relationship, especially if it involves someone we love. Fear of abandonment is our Achilles' heel. And it happens. As we've seen, some women I interviewed lost friendships, even marriages. But it was far more common to have friends egging them on and husbands relieved and delighted to share the financial burden, particularly when their wives' income allowed them to retire.

Still, a woman's newfound independence can be unnerving for men, for the same reason it has been for us—there's insecurity in changing roles. Just as we weren't taught to assert power, men weren't raised to share it. I remember, after a speech I gave to promote my previous book, a man came up afterward to tell me he wasn't going to buy my book for his wife. I bristled at what I took to be unabashed chauvinism, until he explained, "I'm afraid if she reads it, she'll see what a bad job I've been doing with our finances and she'll leave me."

Change is a threat, there's no denying it. Nor can you avoid it, not if you're going to assume your rightful power. The challenge is to assert yourself not only vigilantly and resolutely but also compassionately, sensitive to others' fears, yet always mindful not to sacrifice yourself in order to preserve a relationship. Those who truly love us will eventually celebrate our success and (hopefully) be inspired to live in more deeply satisfying and personally expressive ways themselves.

MONEY IS NOT ALWAYS POWER

Let me make an important distinction: *Money does not give you power.* It allows you to exercise power by providing choices. Your power comes from the choices you make, choices that reflect who you are, not what someone else thinks.

What's important to note is that not all high earners are powerful women. Among those women I interviewed was that slender minority whom we met in chapter 1, the Hard-Driven High Earners, otherwise known as highly dysfunctional overachievers. Except for their incomes, these women had more in common with underearners than with their six-figure sisters. Despite the physical trappings of success, they lived in deprivation, trapped in jobs they disliked or lifestyles that were depleting. They may not have lacked money, but they suffered a severe shortage of time, pleasure, or control over their lives. These hard-driven women were hardly self-determined. They usually blamed someone or something else for their predicaments—their spouses, their bosses, even the money itself—yet expected these very same sources to save or fulfill them. Power denied is always power projected.

In contrast, Successful High Earners empower themselves by living life on their own terms, finding pleasure in their work, their relationships, and the opportunity to serve. As financial adviser Lois Carrier enthusiastically put it, "To do what you love doing and be able to help people and make money, too. Wow, that's unbelievable." No, Lois, that's power.

Powerful *doesn't* mean perfect, however. Successful High Earners occasionally display dysfunctional symptoms. They grapple with fear, time deprivation, and lives out of kilter. They, too, have moments when they feel stuck, dissatisfied, overwhelmed, and incapacitated. Some have valiantly fought feelings of powerlessness stemming from childhood or spousal abuse. Others sometimes still catch themselves shrinking to fit a dusty self-image.

"I've struggled against holding myself back," a very prominent executive confessed. "Once my company approached me to run a division where I'd be managing three men older than myself.

Something inside me said, 'These guys are smarter, more successful; you can't manage them.' I turned down the offer and it was a huge mistake. I've never done that again."

Successful High Earners find it difficult to relinquish their power for long. Sooner rather than later, they'll make a conscious decision to take it right back. The escalating pain of repression can be a compelling incentive to change. To paraphrase Helen Keller, who can be content to crawl once they know what it's like to soar?

STEPPING INTO POWER

I had a long and memorable conversation with a former under-earner who finally hit six figures but at too high a price. Helen became a workaholic, went through a shattering divorce, and suffered a severe bout of depression. When I talked to her, however, those days were long behind her. The story of her healing was that of a woman who claimed her personal power without sacrificing her monetary gain. She did so by following the seven strategies almost to the letter. Her story offers a valuable lesson in applying the strategies to our own lives.

1. Declare an intention.

Helen claimed her power the moment she declared her intention. "I had a very powerful intention to regain my health and still keep my economic independence," she told me. "I'm a strong person, but I never just said, *'I can. I want to. I will.'* When I did, I took my power back."

Over and over again, I saw how those three short sentences said with conviction—*I can! I want to! I will!*—can convert a hapless victim into a powerful woman responsible for creating her own reality. What matters the most is that your intention to profit is compatible with your God-given talents, your authentic aspirations, and your highest good. As writer and poet Audre Lorde once suggested, when you dare to be powerful, using your strengths in the service of your vision, fear becomes a much smaller piece of that larger picture.

2. Let go of the ledge.

But for Helen, that meant getting very clear (and working hard to get that way) about what she wanted and what she was willing to give up. "I had some very harsh beliefs about what it took to be successful, so I had to do a lot of pruning," she told me.

Claiming your power is a Promethean process of individuation and introspection, distinguishing what's true for you from what's been artificially imposed, then *letting go* of what no longer fits. What we think we are—all the shoulds, oughts, musts—gets in the way of what we actually could be. The mark of success is the strength to let go. In fact, I've come to believe that real power is not so much the ability to make something happen as the capacity to make something stop. It is the weeding you do, not just the wages you earn, that gets you back in touch with your power.

3. Get in the game.

As Helen cleared out ancient clutter, it became easier for her to *play the game* the way it's meant to be played. Although Helen was already in the six-figure league, she had become a hard-driven player, forfeiting her power for ruthless ambition. Said Helen, "As I look back, I can say that my goal was to be number one, the most well-known and suc-

cessful woman in my field. If my goal had been to be competent, I think I could have been just as successful but not so
driven. I think that would've made a huge difference." The
difference comes when your goal is to be *your* best, not *the*
best; to put balance in your life, not just money in the bank.

4. *Speak up.*

As soon as she changed her attitude, Helen began to set
boundaries by taking a stand and *speaking up*. She established her priorities and let everyone know what she needed.
She realized that all those times in the past when she had
held her tongue, she had handed over her power.

"I thought of leaving the company. Instead, I set limits,"
Helen recalled. "I told my boss I wasn't getting the support I
expected. He hired an assistant for me. If someone said, 'Can
you get this done by Wednesday?' I would say, 'I'll try, but if
six other things come up I'm not going to stay up all night
Tuesday doing it. I'll get it done by Thursday and not kill
myself. My personal life and my health are too important.'"

5. *Stretch.*

Attempting to actually work less and accomplish as much
was an enormous *stretch* for someone brought up believing
success was impossible without struggle and strain. But as
Helen found out, whenever you exceed your own expectations and achieve more than you imagined you could, you
can't help but see just how powerful you actually are.
However, you can't wait for permission to step beyond
where you are right now. You've got to push yourself to do
what you're not sure you can do, go for the gold with every-

thing you've got, with or without everyone's blessings. As many six-figure women observed, that's how the big boys play this game.

"Sometimes you need balls to get what you want," Helen said, laughing, referring to her determination to scale back her hours but still capture the plum projects. "When I come to a dilemma, I think how would a man handle this. Men take action. They don't ask permission, and they don't stop until someone stops them. Too often women wait for permission or approval."

6. Seek support.

Whenever you buck the system—battling your own resistance as well as the world's—you're going to need all the *support* you can get. That support comes from others who are themselves comfortable with power, but even more important is learning to be supportive of yourself. That notion had never crossed Helen's mind until she went into therapy for depression and realized how poorly she'd been treating herself.

Psychologist Linda Moore points out that neither men nor women have adequately learned the power inherent in taking care of themselves. Women focus on others, men concentrate on work. In both cases, an external emphasis takes a heavy toll. As Linda noted, "When you disconnect from yourself, you disconnect from your power." Quite a few of the women I interviewed made a deliberate effort to find time for themselves, scheduling dates on their calendars for exercise, a massage, or, in Helen's case, "a walk in the woods to stare at a tree."

7. Obey the rules.

Despite her earning six figures, Helen's lifestyle left her teetering on bankruptcy. She finally realized that you can have a fortune at your fingertips, but unless you *obey the three rules*—spend less, save more, invest wisely—you might as well be holding Jell-O. Sooner or later your money and your power will slide right through your fingers. Helen had to learn to care for her money along with her health.

THE FOURTH RULE OF MONEY

There's a fourth rule of money, which allows for the ultimate expression of personal power: Give generously. Here lies the unmatchable joy of making it big. Prosperity offers more opportunity for greater impact. But executing the fourth rule before mastering the first three is like planting crops without preparing the field. The results won't be as bountiful. Giving generously without sufficient savings diminishes the extent of your impact, jeopardizes the quality of your life, and compromises your future security.

EXPRESSING POWER

During our discussion of philanthropy, the majority of the women I interviewed told me something that truly surprised me. They felt the same about giving away money as they did about managing it. The general consensus was that they weren't doing enough. I frequently heard comments like these:

- "I give as much as I can but not as much as I'd like."
- "I write checks to charity but not enough. I wish I had more to give."
- "In my mind, if I can't give huge financial gifts, I'm not giving."

Dollarwise, their charitable contributions were relatively small, the average annual donation less than 5 percent of earnings. As my friend Tracy Gary, the founder of the San Francisco Women's Foundation, told me, "No matter how much a woman has in the bank, she won't give if she feels ignorant, insecure, or anxious about money." How true! With some notable exceptions, the women who felt the least secure about their nest eggs (who had pretty much ignored the first three rules of money), felt equally insecure about their capacity to be charitable and hence gave the least. As Helen said, with obvious remorse, "I've squandered so much, there's not much to give."

But also, many were holding tight to the misconception that they needed a massive bank balance to make any kind of difference. "I give about three thousand dollars a year, not a lot," said one such high earner. "If I had tons of money I'd love to give it to women entrepreneurs who have a dream, but I'd need real money, at least seven hundred thousand dollars. You can't make a big impact unless you're making walloping sums."

She obviously hadn't met Carol Anderson. On Carol's fiftieth birthday, this self-employed consultant asked her friends not to bring presents and instead donate to what would become Rebellious Dreamers, a nonprofit she was forming to give financial support and mentoring to women who had forsaken their dreams. "Success isn't if she goes on to do her dream," Carol explained. Success is her having the chance to find out, so she won't be wondering all her life." Because of Carol and her friends, an aspiring singer cut a promotional CD and a waitress hoping to be a photographer bought camera equipment and took classes. "It's changed their lives," said Carol. And without walloping sums.

Don't get me wrong. Every woman I interviewed was very conscious of using her checkbook (along with volunteering her time and expertise) to leave her mark on the world. Many bemoaned the fact that they couldn't do more, but they all contributed what they felt they could afford. They consulted pro bono to nonprofits and mentored kids in the ghetto. They sat on boards and organized fund-raisers. They paid off their parents' mortgage, a friend's college tuition, and the hospital bills for a child born with disabilities. They set up scholarship funds and supported food banks. They contributed to all kinds of causes but were partial to programs for women, children, and the elderly. And they encouraged others to do the same.

They all gave for basically the same reasons: They feel blessed and want to give back; giving brings them great joy; they believe that spiritually money given away always comes back; and because, as entrepreneur Gun Denhart colorfully phrased it, "Money is like manure. If you pile it up it stinks. But if you spread it around, it does a lot of good."

Some of the women I spoke to were engaged in incredibly lofty, compassionate, and creative acts of kindness. For example, Abby, an attorney, uses all her vacation time supervising elections in the Balkans, setting up Internet service in Kosovo, or volunteering with the refugee resettlement program in New York. She even brought her Balkan interpreter to the United States to study when he was about to be drafted into the Serbian army. "I got my congresswoman to help me get a visa for him. I wrote a check for twelve thousand dollars to pay for his tuition."

Judith Wicks, who owns the White Dog Café in Philadelphia, routinely takes customers and employees to Nicaragua, Vietnam,

Russia, Cuba, even the ghettos of her own city, because, she said, "If we want world peace, we need real relationships with real people." She nicknamed the program Eating with the Enemy. "I think the problems of the world could be solved if people understood we're all connected. They'd take better care of each other," she told me. "People are literally transformed on these tours."

Gun Denhart uses her catalog company, Hanna Anderson, as a platform to support needy children by donating 5 percent of the profits. Every catalog carries a blurb about a different program that helps children. "Do you know that twenty-five percent of the children in this country live below poverty level?" Gun said. "My heart goes out to these kids. I look at my own children and how fortunate they are. It's really great to help others."

Susan Davis founded her firm, Capital Missions Company, with the express purpose of "making a profit while making a difference," by creating networks of socially responsible investors who invest for "triple bottom line" returns (financial, social, and environmental). "If CMC wasn't profitable, how could it expect to have impact?" Susan asked, knowing full well it takes money to improve human life and change the system, as well as to get people's attention.

Hedge-fund manager Renee Haugerud started a children's educational fund, because, as she likes to say, "Women have been socialized to be Florence Nightingale. I tell women if they want to change the world, if they want to help, do it by making a lot of money, then create a foundation for philanthropic giving."

THIS IS WHAT IT'S ALL ABOUT

Each one of us has the capacity to reshape the world in a myriad of ways, even more so if we're making a good living. Income, influence, and autonomy are very much related. A financially independent woman—one who is at ease with abundance and receptive to the freedom it brings—has the wherewithal needed for sculpting her life as well as bettering humanity.

I truly believe that when enough women claim their power, collectively we'll have the resources, values, vision, and sensitivity to change the world, to heal the planet. Many years ago, Louis Aragon, a poet of the French Resistance, prophesied, "Woman is the future of man." More recently, after conducting a survey for the *Ladies' Home Journal,* the sociologist Madelyn Hochstein made a similar proclamation: "The rising influence of women will be one of the most powerful transformative forces of the 21st century."

To rise to the challenge, however, we ourselves must be transformed. That means enlarging our field of vision by thinking much bigger than we do now about how much more we can make, how much more we can do, and how much more we can be.

I'll never forget how Brooke O'Shay described her shock when, after agonizing for days, she finally confronted her boss about a promotion to six figures, and he immediately agreed. At that moment Brooke had a revelation so common to successful women that I've dubbed it the *High Earners' Epiphany:* "If I had known how much more power I have over my existence, I wonder if my entire life would have been different?"

Each and every one of us has so much more power to govern our life than we can possibly imagine.

The poet Mark Nepo tells us that within each of us the extraordinary is quietly waiting beneath the skin of all that's ordinary. As I reflect on my conversations with these high-powered women, I realize the truth of that statement. This, I believe, is the most significant secret their stories convey, as well as the gauntlet they've dropped at your feet. By their words and their actions, they're saying to you:

Release the extraordinary buried inside you. Awaken the Goddess within. Every time you leave the beaten path and aim for the exceptional, every time you silence your fear and speak with your own voice, every time you stop acting small and start taking up space, you are owning your power and emancipating others to follow in your footsteps.

Together these seven strategies should enable you to do just that—expand your potential, become all you can be, create more abundance, and share it with others. Together the strategies will prepare you to become the transformative force you were meant to be—perhaps as a six-figure earner, but unquestionably as a more powerful woman. And the world will be so much better for it.

APPENDIX

RESOURCES
(BOOKS AND WEBSITES)

- Sources of salary range information
    American Almanac of Jobs and Salaries
    National Association of Colleges & Employers: Salary Survey
    www.jobtrack.com
    www.jobsmart.com
    www.careercity.com
    www.paypeopleright.com
    www.townonline.com/working
    www.bls.gov/opub/cwc/cwhome.htm
    www.salary.com

- My favorite savings, spending, and debt reduction sites
    www.financialrecovery.com
    www.debtorsanonymous.org

www.asec.org

www.123Debt.com

www.betterbudgeting.com

www.ivillagemoneylife.com

- My favorite women's financial sites

    www.msmoney.com

    www.cassandrasrevenge.com

    www.womensinvest.com

    www.wfn.com

    www.allwomeninvest.com

- My favorite personal finance sites

    www.fool.com

    www.money.com

    www.quicken.com

    www.kiplingers.com

    www.smartmoney.com

    www.ihatefinancialplanning.com

- My all-time favorite money books

    The Richest Man in Babylon by George S. Clason (Plume, 1926)—As one critic said about this book, published in 1926, it "ranks . . . among the important business preachments of modern times." I agree.

    Money Is My Friend by Phil Laut (Trinity Publications, 1978)—Another timeless text that goes way beyond the nuts and bolts and will change the way you think about money.

    Personal Finance for Dummies by Eric Tyson (IDG Books, 1994)—I recommend all the "dummy" books written by

Tyson, a noted financial writer. He knows how to turn a complicated subject into easy and (yes!) fun reading.

Getting to Yes by Roger Fisher, William Ury, and Bruce Patton (Penguin, 1991)—Based on the work of the Harvard Negotiation Project, this has become the bible of win-win negotiating. There's also a workbook by the same title.

Earn What You Deserve by Jerrold J. Mundis (Bantam Books, 1995)—Written by a recovered underearner, this perennial seller is forthright, practical, and transformational. I also recommend *How to Get Out of Debt, Stay Out of Debt and Live Prosperously* (Bantam Books, 1988) by the same author.

Rich Dad, Poor Dad by Robert Kiyosaki (Warner Books, 2000)—Lately, publishers are churning out financial books faster than the mint prints money, but this one stands out from the masses. The author uses an entertaining parable to explain basic financial principals.

The MoneyMinder Workbook by Karen McCall (Financial Recovery Institute, 2000)—The updated edition of the Financial Recovery Workbook is even better than the original, which I thought was pretty terrific. I also recommend Karen's latest book: *It's Your Money: Achieving Financial Well-Being* (Chronicle Books, 2000).

- Inspirational classics

    When you need a megadose of motivation, pick up one of these classics (recommended by the women I interviewed):

    Think and Grow Rich by Napoleon Hill (Fawcett, 1960)

    The Seven Habits of Highly Effective People by Stephen Covey (Simon & Schuster, 1991)

Awaken the Giant Within and *Unlimited Power* by Tony Robbins (Fireside, 1993 and Fireside, 1997)

Creative Visualization by Shakti Gawain (Bantam, 1983)

The Dynamic Laws of Prosperity by Catherine Ponder (DeVorss & Co., 1972)

TIPS FOR GETTING
OUT OF DEBT

1. Make the decision: NO MORE DEBT.
   - Cut up your credit cards.
   - Pay for everything in cash only.

2. Don't be vague about money. Develop a spending plan.
   - Track your daily spending. Buy a small notebook for your purse. Write down every penny you spend, from a parking fee to a pack of gum.
   - Put all your expenses into categories (home, food, clothing, self-care, health care, transportation, etc.).
   - Decide where you can cut expenses. It's better to shave small amounts from several categories.
   - Be creative. Ask yourself: How can I reduce spending in this category and still get my needs met? For

example, stop buying books or renting videos and get them at the library.

- Use this extra money for debt repayment.

3. Set up a debt-repayment plan.

- Go to www.quicken.com to figure out a debt-reduction plan. You can also check your credit report. (If you don't have a computer, visit a library, a community center, or a local college.)
- Consolidate high-interest loans onto one lower-interest-rate credit card. DO NOT charge anything on this card. Cancel your other cards immediately. (Find and apply for lower-interest credit cards on www.quicken.com.)
- Contact creditors. Explain your situation and payment plan. Keep written records of conversations.
- Pay off the creditor with the highest interest rate first.

4. Start saving.

- Get a jar. Every day, put $2 into the jar, plus all your spare change. By the end of the month, you'll have more than $70.
- Use coupons and rebates. Add the money to your jar.
- Save a portion of *all* income, including bonuses, gifts, and refunds, and put it in the jar.
- Ask your bank to automatically withdraw $5 to $10 every month, or whatever you can afford, from your payroll check or checking account and put it into a savings account.

5. Get help. It can be very tough to get out of debt alone.

- Call Consumer Credit Counselors (800-777-PLAN). They will help you develop a payment plan, talk to your credi-

tors, even negotiate lower interest rates. And you can do it
all over the phone.

- Attend Debtors Anonymous meetings. Call the local
  DA chapter, or Alcoholics Anonymous, listed in the
  phone book.
- Find a buddy who is also trying to get out of debt
  and support each other.
- Talk to family members. Family support is crucial.

6. Deal with your emotions.
   - Examine your early messages about money. Childhood
     experiences, cultural attitudes, and family behaviors have
     an extraordinary influence on how we deal with money.
   - Stop beating yourself up for getting into debt. This
     perpetuates the spending cycle. When you feel bad, you
     spend more to feel good.

INVESTING BASICS:
WEALTH BUILDING 101
(A VERY QUICK LESSON)

There are only five places to invest your money:

1. Stocks
2. Bonds
3. Real estate
4. Commodities
5. Cash, or cash equivalents

These "places" are called *asset classes.*

- *Stock is ownership in a company.* When you buy a hundred shares of IBM, you become a partial, albeit small, owner of the giant firm.
- *A bond is an IOU.* When you buy a bond, the issuer of that bond, usually a corporation or a government or its agency,

promises to pay you back in full, plus interest, by a certain date.

- *Real estate* includes *land and/or buildings*.
- *Commodities* are *tangible goods* such as grains, metals, and foods.
- *Cash equivalents are highly liquid (easily converted to cash), guarantee a full return, and pay very low interest.* Examples include money market funds, certificates of deposit, and short-term Treasury bills.

Of these five places to invest:

- Real estate is illiquid and usually too much work for neophyte investors. So, if you're a beginner, let's scratch that.
- Commodities are way too risky, complicated, and sophisticated for the average person. They're out, too.
- Stocks, bonds, and cash are really the only three asset classes you need to understand, at least initially.

There are only two ways to invest. As an *owner* or a *loaner*. That means:

- When you buy a share of stock, you own a piece of a company.
- When you buy a bond, you loan money to the issuer of the bond.

Other differences between stocks and bonds include:

- Stocks can make more money. But stocks have more volatility. As sure as a stock goes up, it will also go down.

- Bonds won't fluctuate nearly as much. They pay interest. And, if you buy good bonds, you'll most likely get back your original investment.

Here are a few reasons why you should own stocks:

- Stocks go up and down in value more than bonds, but they will make you more money over time.
- Stocks have risen an average of 11 percent a year.
- Bonds have returned 5.2 percent a year.
- Treasuries have gained about 3 percent a year.
- Inflation averages 3 to 4 percent a year.
- Stocks have earned more than seven percentage points above inflation, while bonds have offered only around two points more and Treasuries barely break even.
- If you want to protect your money from inflation and taxes, you need to have some of it in the stock market.

You'll want to invest in all three—stocks, bonds, and cash:

- Stocks give you growth.
- Bonds give you income.
- Cash gives you a safe place to park your money for emergencies or future investments.

When deciding where to invest your money, consider the following tips:

- *Asset allocation* refers to how you divide your money among the five asset classes.

- *Diversification* refers to how you divide your money in each particular asset class.
- The most important investment decision you make will be how to diversify and allocate your assets.
- There's no one way to diversify that's right for everyone. The decision depends on your age, your income, when you need your money, and your risk tolerance.
- You can invest in individual stocks and bonds; however, it's expensive to buy enough shares of stocks or individual bonds to be diversified.
- You don't need a lot of money to invest in mutual funds.
- A mutual fund pools your money with other people's money to buy a diversified portfolio of stocks, bonds, or whatever investment the particular fund emphasizes. Also, a professional will manage your money.
- The easiest way to begin investing in stocks is with this diversification:
  1. a large cap (large companies) mutual fund (try an S&P index fund)
  2. a small cap (small companies) mutual fund
  3. an international fund (outside the United States)
- Do your research before you buy; it's easy to do on the Internet.
- Max out your tax-deferred retirement accounts first.

INDEX